Libraries *in a* world *of* cultural change

Liz Greenhalgh & Ken Worpole
with Charles Landry

First published in 1995 by UCL Press

UCL Press Limited
University College London
Gower Street
London WC1E 6BT

The name of University College London (UCL) is a registered
trade mark used by UCL Press with the consent of the owner.

ISBNs:
1-85728-468-2 HB
1-85728-469-0 PB

British Library Cataloguing-in-Publication Data
A CIP catalogue record for this book is available from the British Library.

Library of Congress Cataloging-in-Publication Data are available.

Front cover: "Croydon Library 1995"
by Larraine Worpole.

Typeset in Times New Roman.
Printed and bound by
Page Bros (Norwich) Ltd, England.

Contents

Preface   v
Acknowledgements   ix

Part 1: Introduction

1 Introduction   3

2 Key concepts   10

Part 2: Institutions in crisis

3 The end of enlightenment   19

4 The changing role of public institutions   26

5 The modern library network   37

6 Political invisibility   43

Part 3: The "libraryness" of libraries

7 What makes libraries special?   51

8 The era of light and glass   60

Part 4: Spheres of influence

9 Libraries and urban vitality   73

CONTENTS

10 The invisible web: the public library and social policy   89

11 Education and life-long learning   100

12 Information and the right to know   112

13 Other worlds: libraries, fiction and popular reading   130

Part 5: Tomorrow's world

14 Past, present and future   139

15 The modern state and new meanings of the public   150

Notes   169
Bibliography   175
Index   179

Preface

Comedia is an independent research consultancy, specializing in cultural and urban policy issues. It began working primarily in Britain, but in recent years has been involved in an increasing number of European projects, as well as working collaboratively with other research, academic and policy organizations in Australia and North America.

Much of the early work in Britain was around issues of developing new media, particularly at a local and regional level, and Comedia was involved in researching and publishing pioneering studies of community radio, independent publishing and bookselling, independent film and video production, as well as researching and publishing studies of the record industry, the theatre industry and other areas of modern cultural production, distribution and reception. While much cultural policy at the time emphasized production, particularly by new cultural interest groups, Comedia was more concerned with questions of effective distribution and communication. An interest in marketing, and a concern for developing audiences for these new cultural forms and products, was an early sphere of interest and a subject of detailed research and development.

In the 1980s, Comedia's work became much more involved in understanding and developing the links between cultural policy and urban policy, particularly around issues of urban regeneration, inward investment into towns and cities, and a realization that questions of cultural identity were at the centre not only of individual lifestyles, but of the lives of towns and cities themselves – especially as the latter appeared to be losing their historic, industrial, economic and social identities in a welter of standardized town centre retail development. And where British policy-makers seemed to be being urged to adopt, sometimes wholesale, North American models of retail-led urban regeneration, Comedia researchers were already aware that European models might be more rewarding to understand and adapt to British conditions, particularly concerning an attention to the quality of public space and traditions of civic culture in urban renewal. Naturally, this detailed interest in specific towns and cities led to a close co-operation with local authorities, and an awareness not only of the importance of local democracy and decision making in strengthening local distinctiveness, but also of the unique flavour of local traditions and services – which were (and still are) in danger of being lost as government economic centralism continues largely unabated. It seemed bad enough that many town centre retailing and manufacturing processes had become nothing more than "branch economies" of national and international companies, let alone that local government and other civic institutions would themselves become direct instruments of central government policy, and lose all local powers and opportunities for strengthening local identity.

Towards the end of the 1980s there was a general perception, which to a degree Comedia's own work had anticipated, that "the retail revolution" had failed to deliver all the urban vitality and economic renewal that it had promised. In fact, British town centres seemed to be dying, rather than achieving a second golden age. Shopping, it seemed, was not enough. The principal people working at Comedia at the time – Franco Bianchini, Liz Greenhalgh, Charles Landry and Ken Worpole – approached the Gulbenkian Foundation with a proposal to study the perceived social and cultural crisis of town centres in Britain, and not only received a sympathetic hearing, but also a development grant to get what transpired to be the first of a series of national studies – principally undertaken in partnership with a network of local authorities – off the ground.

This study of the "economic, social and cultural life" of 12 town centres in Britain, undertaken between 1989 and 1991, was published as the *Out of hours* report in May 1991. It received wide coverage and considerable interest, particularly within the planning and urban policy professions and networks. A book version of that study, *Towns for people*, written by Ken Worpole, was published in 1992.[1] Not only had the study been illuminating and challenging, it had also provided a way of working with local authorities and funding bodies that proved to be immensely rewarding, cost-effective and intellectually stimulating to all involved. Case studies were undertaken in each local authority area, thus providing locally specific research, but funds were also available for researching national and even international trends and examples of best practice.

. It was the *Out of hours* study that raised many of the issues that have been explored since, particularly questions regarding the nature and quality of public space, the public sphere, civic culture and the nature of modern citizenship – all difficult but pressing questions. But the study also "discovered", or identified, particular spaces and places – notably public libraries, parks and other more locally specific civic cultures – that still seemed to be thriving, despite the pressures from outside, spaces and places where it was still possible to note a liveliness, conviviality and sense of mutual respect (rather than the slightly suspect elixir of "community") that was thought to have been entirely expunged by consumerism and the compulsion to turn every economic, social and cultural relationship into a commercial transaction. The critical appreciation of public libraries that follows is the outcome of that long-term understanding.

Acknowledgements

As this book grew out of the Comedia report on public libraries, acknowledgements and thanks are due to those who made the original research possible. They were, in their capacity as Advisory Board members: Franco Bianchini, Frank Boyd, Jean Carr, Robin Clement, Sarah Dunant, Bill McAlister, Kenneth May, Geoff Mulgan, Geoffrey Smith, Rosemary Stones and Ben Whitaker. Thanks are also due to members of the original project Steering Group, and the library authorities they represented, not just for their involvement at the national level but for their close involvement with the case studies: Geoff Allen, Janet Barker, Pat Coleman, Carleton Earl, Carol Holmes, Mike Hughes, Linda Piercey, Ian Rawlinson, Patrick Roach, John Saunders; and to colleagues at the Library and Information Services Council (Northern Ireland): Harry Carson, Russell Farrow and Ian Montgomery.

For contributions to the series of seminars organized during the course of the original research, we would like to thank again Stephen Greenberg (*Architects Journal*), Hilary Hammond (Director of Arts and Libraries, Norfolk County Council), Hugo Hinsley (Architectural Association, London), Bob McNulty (Partners for Liveable Communities, USA), Wendy Mason (Rivington Street Studios, London) and Dr Judy White (Centre for Urban & Regional Studies, Birmingham University). Thanks are also due to those who contributed to the series of Working Papers, including Chris Batt, Alistair Black, Geoff Mulgan, Dave Muddiman, Rebecca O'Rourke and Keiran Phelan. The study was greatly helped by the interest and support of John Sumsion of the Library Information and Statistics Unit at Loughborough University of

Technology. And thanks are due to Owen Kelly and Naseem Khan who have also contributed to the book.

Many others, unfortunately too numerous to mention, gave their help by agreeing to be interviewed, sending us papers, articles and bibliographies, and through many other kindnesses, which we gratefully acknowledge here. The project would simply not have happened were it not for the support of the bodies who funded it, and so sincere thanks to David Carrington of the Baring Foundation, Geoffrey Smith and David Landale of TC Farries and the Landale Trust, Robin Clement of London Planning Advisory Council and of course Ben Whitaker at the Calouste Gulbenkian Foundation, and to their respective trustees. Thanks are also due to Simon Frith, Michael Green and Jim McGuigan who made valuable comments on the report and, finally, to Justin Vaughan of UCL Press who commissioned this book, which we hope fulfils his original expectations.

PART 1

Introduction

CHAPTER 1

Introduction

The Comedia study was the first independent study of public libraries in Britain since the Second World War, and this book is largely the result of that detailed research, which was finalized in 1993. We wanted to look at public libraries in greater detail because, as outsiders, we regarded them as continuing to exhibit signs of considerable success: success in maintaining a wide cross-section of the population as regular users; success in continuing to keep abreast of new media forms – records, tapes, CDs, videos, open learning materials; success in steering a fine line between populist consumerism and elitist cultural exclusivity; success in maintaining a distinctive social and public space, and success too in maintaining particular and distinctive standards of public architecture when and where there were opportunities for new buildings. But, paradoxically, librarians saw things otherwise. They perceived continuing – and in some cases even terminal – crisis.

This book is about that crisis: illusory, perceived or real. It is about understanding that however successful public libraries may appear to be to users and outsiders, and indeed in many places they seemed to be prospering, the political and fiscal context within which they were and are provided – by local government on the basis of free, universal provision, paid for out of direct taxation – was most certainly in deep trouble, and possibly nearing an end. Were public libraries, we asked, living on borrowed time?

There were other elements to the "crisis" too: a flurry of articles in the press about the reduction in opening hours in some town centre libraries, particularly in London; the occasional fanning into flames of a moral panic about "political correctness" and whether public libraries should or should not stock Little Black Sambo stories; but also a general sense that local government was seriously under attack, and that libraries would inevitably suffer as a result. The 1980s also saw a determined attack by the government on the professions themselves, which were portrayed as conspiracies against the free market, and along with doctors, solicitors, teachers and others, public librarians were challenged to justify their "protectionist" professional practices against the potential greater efficiency and better service to the users or consumers, of services managed, marketed and delivered with greater flexibility, and with less hierarchical job structures and greater competition. In the endless turmoil of continuing local government reorganization and internal restructuring, self-contained library departments were variously incorporated, absorbed, annexed to and at worst hijacked by larger departments or directorates, occasionally with gains in political status and departmental effectiveness, but often with a loss of confidence and a down-grading of status and political visibility. The public may not have noticed this crisis, but librarians did. All of this made the value of an independent evaluation even more timely.

An independent viewpoint

It was realized from the earlier study of town centres that an independent assessment of the problems currently facing public services, and the professional traditions that sustain them, could only help, even if some of the diagnoses and subsequent prescriptions seemed critical. It is quite sobering to realize that there had been no independent evaluation of public library services in Britain for possibly fifty years, or, to put it another way, for more than two generations. Of course the library profession itself had continued to conduct its own internal reviews, publish and disseminate differing points of view about the way forward, commission user research and so on. But this was all done within the habits, professional languages and belief systems of librarians themselves – the inside looking out, so to speak, rather than the outside looking in. All institutions need both perspectives.

For it was not only a critical, independent eye that a research team put together by Comedia could provide, but it was also the insights and intellectual contributions supplied by a range of other disciplines. The Comedia team, together with its Advisory Board and those experts commissioned to provide the study Working Papers, in fact included not a single librarian, but instead contained economists, sociologists, literary critics, urban planners, media analysts, philosophers, commercial marketing experts and local government strategists, all of whom were delighted to rise to the challenge of bringing their own professional disciplines to bear upon the problems of the public library network, in the wider interest of change, development and renewal. It was at times a bumpy ride. Many of them had not given much thought to public libraries before: sometimes they were delighted with what they found; often they were shocked. For these were people who had perhaps changed professions (and certainly institutions or companies) several times in their lives, who were constantly in contact with developments abroad, heavily reliant on a daily flow of market or contextual information and for whom constant performance-monitoring was a fact of daily life. Demographic change, technological change, a sensitivity to both the national and global political situation, an awareness in the latest management thinking, in systems analysis, in organizational flexibility and responsiveness were for many of them preconditions of effective provision and decision making. Yet they found themselves looking at a public institution that preferred development by accretion, valued continuity above flexibility, preferred to consolidate a known audience above developing "new markets", and that valued professional loyalty and integrity often above individual careers.

Independent evaluation also brings opportunities for new connections to be made. Comedia's long experience with the economic arguments for the role of cultural resources in urban renewal was an unfamiliar argument to many in the library world; connections with planning arguments and policies, with economic development strategies, seemed only natural to the Comedia team, but these were sometimes new arguments within the library profession.

Organizational insights also can be brought in from other fields and disciplines. Again Comedia's history of work with the voluntary sector, with the newer networking paradigms of cultural development, was able to be utilized in the service of critically understanding how public library services organized themselves to deliver the services they did, and whether the existing organizational forms were adequate to the work needing to be done in the future. We were also able to move towards particular conclusions about the current public library service, and make recommendations for some of the directions it might take, without self-interest. Too often internal management reviews or policy debates are tunnelled towards conclusions that were desired or anticipated from the beginning, as much as certain kinds of public consultation are simply mechanisms designed to win consent to decisions already made.

Towards the end of the study, members of the team found themselves at times as public advocates for the very best that the public library service had to offer, better advocates in some cases than librarians themselves, who could no longer see the wood for the trees, or effectively understand just how important what they did was to other people, and the many direct and indirect impacts on the economic, social and cultural life that were actually achieved. Indeed, at a number of presentations made to professional library audiences, librarians themselves admitted that they not only had not realized the full extent of the strategic importance of the library service to the quality of urban life, but also had failed to convince or inspire the outside world to take their work seriously.

All these arguments attest, we feel, to the value of independent, critical research and policy development. Yet if public libraries are so important, as we concluded they are, then we also believe that they are too important to be left solely to librarians. The case for the public library as a general good is now a matter of concern for all, for those who believe in universal rights and opportunities for self-improvement, as well as those who believe in the specificities of local identity, of cultural minority rights, and of individual development and self-worth. The library is not only a powerful symbol of the past, but also a potential beacon or landmark for the future.

Borrowed time?

Yet such public debate as there currently is about libraries usually takes the form of a nostalgia for a "world we have lost" – memories of libraries from childhood rather than what libraries actually are now and could be in the future. And while in many of Britain's towns and cities, libraries play a significant role in information policy and cultural renewal – with on-line business services, economic development initiatives, open learning and adult literacy schemes, local history projects, the encouragement of early reading and support for quality children's fiction – in other places the public library is failing to adapt to new conditions and could disappear as commercial forces overwhelm it.

This book is based on a large-scale, national research project involving detailed research throughout the United Kingdom, as well as on interviews with more than a thousand people – library providers, library users, policy analysts, social forecasters, information and technology experts, publishers and booksellers. It seeks to take a fresh and sometimes critical look at the future of the public library.

A preliminary report, *Borrowed time?* – which we regarded as a "Green Paper" consultative document – was published in June 1993 to considerable national and international interest.[1] Among the many findings that emerged from that research, and that are examined in detail in this book, are the following critical issues:

– Libraries are still popular institutions. About a third of the UK population uses public libraries regularly. Up to half of the population uses them occasionally. They provide an information network or "national grid", linked at local, regional and national levels. Yet there is no real national strategic thinking. Without this the network could atrophy and possibly disappear.

– Along with all other "public" institutions, public libraries were having to develop a new rationale, management and funding system to survive in a mixed economy. Some seemed capable of adapting to these new conditions; some did not.

– Despite popular mythology, public library services in Britain have in general enjoyed growth in recent years, although opening hours have been reduced in a number of places. There are some famous exceptions to this pattern of growth, particularly in London boroughs, but nationally more than 300 new libraries were built in the 1980s.

– While book issues have been slowly declining, other uses of the library are increasing – for information, for study, as homework centres, for literary events and other community activities. Unfortunately, librarians are often failing to articulate, monitor or even promote these other uses to the wider world.

– In many, if not all of Britain's town centres, the public library is one of the most accessible and open public institutions, and often acts as a focal point for local civic life.

- Public libraries have suffered a loss of visibility in the political realm through having no national body to represent their interests. As a result they have often been on the receiving end of policy developments such as local management of schools or care in the community – which have had major impacts on them but with little or no advance consultation.
- While other cultural institutions – theatres, opera houses, concert halls – were regarded as key elements in programmes of urban regeneration in the 1980s, public libraries (usually responsible for generating more city centre activity than all the others) were excluded.

These are mostly institutional issues – sometimes of great success, sometimes of significant failure. What this book attempts to do is to understand the richnesses of the public library tradition from an independent perspective, and to try to map out the future of the public library within the exigencies of a rapidly changing, turbulent and competitive political world. The public library has many friends – but not enough in "high places". It offers many services – but it isn't quite sure which are more important than others. It has a very long and valued history – but we live in an age in which long-standing institutions can suddenly disappear for ever. Many urgent decisions will need to be made if the public library is to adapt to the new demands of a new millennium. It is hoped that this book will help that process.

New arguments

This book draws on all the work that went into the original consultative report – which used only a fraction of the material produced – including responses to the case studies and to the nine Working Papers, responses to *Borrowed time?*, and on the results of many seminars and discussions held over the past two years. What it attempts to do – which the report could not – is elaborate the intellectual and technical arguments for public library provision in the light of the enormous social, demographic and political changes all developed countries are living through at the end of the twentieth century. It is therefore more than just a book about libraries, it is about how the public intellectual realm will be sustained and developed (not necessarily a foregone conclusion) in a period that is seeing massive developments in electronic communications, in powerful pressures towards consumer individualism, and in increasing disparities not only of wealth but also of access to information. It is about whether future societies will be based on a "need to know", "can afford to know" or on "a right to know" basis. Public libraries could make the difference.

CHAPTER 2

Key concepts

This book, along with much of the recent work of Comedia on public space and civic cultures, is informed by a number of concepts and terms which, because they are so frequently to be found in the text, are worth elaborating or signposting here. Dictionary-type definitions of course are never enough and, as with so many words and ideas, their meaning always depends on the nuances of the contexts in which they are used. Yet we find these conceptual frameworks and terms so useful – if occasionally improperly understood – that we wish at least to try and explain how they have been used. A considerable intellectual debt here is owed to Raymond Williams's *Keywords*.[1]

"Public"

The definition of the term "public" is historically broad-ranging and it is used in everyday language and in this book in a number of ways. Indeed, it is a central term. It includes "the public sphere", "public realm", "public space", "public building", "public interest", "public access" and of course "public library". The word "public" embraces a multifaceted set of meanings, including "concerning the people as a whole", "open to all" "maintained at the expense of the community", "serving the community" and "for the use of the community". Synonyms for these uses encompass "civic", "common" or "communal", "general", "social", "universal", "widespread", "not restricted", "accessible" and "not private".

Often, "public" is contrasted with the terms "individual", "private" and even "self-interest". Over the last decade, "public" has in fact more or less exclusively been contrasted to "private" and there has been an implication that "private" is somehow by definition good and "public" by definition bad or at least inefficient. There are, of course, many aspects of private and self-interested behaviour that should remain so, but equally there are many areas, such as education, where "public funding" in the sense of "maintained at the expense of the community" and "public access" in the sense of "open to all" are of benefit to both individuals and society as a whole. The issue is precisely how public and private interests can be maximized, as is now being witnessed in the increasing popularity of true public–private partnerships.

The public sphere

Chief among all the uses of the word "public" in this study is the notion of *the public sphere*. This concept, which is also often termed *the public realm*, derives largely from the work of the German philosopher Jürgen Habermas, still alive today, whose seminal work *The structural transformation of the public sphere*, published in Germany in the early 1960s, was not published in an English translation until 1989.[2] This book charted the growth of a public realm of debate, argument, contractual rights, and rational bureaucracy that grew up in Europe in post-monarchical societies, and in which the very notion that political development might be based on rational discussion first gained the ascendancy. Habermas drew his conclusions from a study of British, French and German history, although Britain was a clear focus as it had been the first to abolish censorship – a clear precondition of the emergence of an independent public sphere. The other characteristics of this autonomous realm were free speech, a free press and the right to a free assembly.

The term is still used today to discuss that realm of public debate – newspapers, television, lobby groups, voluntary organizations, political parties, books, and of course libraries – where public ideas, opinions, values and beliefs are shaped and modified. For Habermas, the public sphere he most fully elaborated was that of European bourgeois culture, and recent critics have pointed out the weakness of this concept in not

11

dealing with the separate cultures and sub-cultures of, for example, working-class movements and organizations, of the life of the home (and the views of women), of the impact of the mass media and the breakdown of the strict demarcation lines between "high" and "popular" culture, and so on. It is not difficult to see how central the development of libraries – radical, independent, commercial and finally public – has been to the development of this public sphere of argument and debate.

Finally, for Habermas and his followers, the public sphere neither belongs to the state nor to the free market but is independent of both, although it contains elements of the effects of both. It thus avoids the contemporary polarities – particularly relevant to current debates about the funding, management and autonomy of public libraries – between the political camps of old-fashioned statism or the excesses of the free market lobby.

Public space

The question of the value and social function of public space – particularly within towns and cities – is another one of Comedia's principal concerns in recent years and has informed much of its own research and policy formulation which has been indebted, in turn, to the work of American sociologists and urbanists such as Jane Jacobs, Richard Sennett and Sharon Zukin.[3] The term "public space" is a description of the physical manifestation of those places – libraries, parks, streets, squares and other covered or open spaces – which people can use as a right, for free, and which are in many ways felt to be held in common ownership and open to all. As the vitality of streets and street cultures has been killed by cars, as shopping streets have become displaced by private covered malls, as museums and other once free venues have been forced to impose entrance charges, so the opportunities to wander, to browse, to stand and chat, to sit and watch the world go by become squeezed and constrained. This, we feel, is one of the pre-eminent values of the public library, as neutral space, as democratic, non-sectarian territory. Urban cultures need free space as much as they need working space and selling space: the life of towns needs convivial public spaces.

12

The public service remit

Many commentators continue to draw an analogy between the role of the public library service in Britain – its management, funding and intellectual ethos – and that of public service broadcasting. This seems to us quite valid. Radio and television in Britain were established as a public service, funded by a licence fee, and managed by the British Broadcasting Corporation (established in 1927) under a Royal Charter.[4] This contrasts, for example, with the USA where radio and television broadcasting from the outset were funded by advertising and subject to no programming constraints or obligations by the state or the political process. The public service ethos in Britain combined a triple obligation to "inform, educate and entertain". Such regulatory obligations still apply to commercial television and radio in Britain, although commercial radio today is handled by the Independent Radio Authority with what is termed a "lighter touch". Channel 4, for example, has an explicit policy remit to cater for minority interests, to be innovative, and to have a strong educational commitment. Although the public library service has itself no explicit policy objectives nationally, the Library Advisory Council (for England) in 1973 claimed that public libraries functioned within four main areas of responsibility: education, information, culture and leisure. Librarians and library assistants in our opinion, based on our many interviews with them, still see themselves operating within a public service remit, rather than within a wholly consumer-led rationale.

Civil society

Related to the public sphere is the notion of civil society, again a description of an historical formation of a rational bureaucracy, subject to the law, that mediated between the state and pressure groups of all kinds. Today the term seems to be used – and it is the way we have used it – to denote the idea of a political realm that is based on rights and responsibilities over and above personal interest, mediated through the institutions of political parties, pressure groups, local government, parliament, and so on, but with a view to a greater good than the mere sense that society is simply the aggregation of an infinite number of personal needs and interests.

Cultural diversity

The concept of cultural diversity is based on the recognition that modern societies are much more cosmopolitan than ever before, as a result of global movements of migration and transmigration over the past 300 years, and that it is no longer possible to talk of historic or essentialist national cultural identities. Modern societies are continually in transition and are becoming so at a faster rate than before. They are made up of a multiplicity of national, regional, class and ethnic identities and interests, all of which have their own cultural traditions.

Life-long learning

Education is bursting the banks of institutional provision and happening everywhere in society today, as and when people require it. Job skills are no longer the property of the company (as in the days of Fordist mass production when people were treated as "hands") but now become the property – and responsibility – of individuals to own and develop, as they change jobs or skills many times in their lives.

In future, the public realm could be quintessentially an educational realm. Not in the conventional understanding that education is about schools, but in the sense of the massive expansion of further and higher education and life-long learning. Interestingly, some cities and boroughs – Liverpool particularly, Southwark, Ealing among others – have staked their plans for urban regeneration and civic renewal on the growth of city centre or urban heartland educational expansion.

The facts support these arguments: the Open University is now Britain's largest single teaching institution; most universities now enrol thousands of part-time students of all ages; Ford and Nissan both have extensive open learning programmes and schemes to encourage individual skills' development; the University of the Third Age is now established. Some 6 million adults are involved in some form of adult education. A culture of self-development based on life-long learning is clearly expanding.

The right to know

The role of the library in providing information services is in large part to empower citizens, and by this means to help bridge the gap between the "information rich" and "information poor". Genuine self-improvement and empowerment involve a strong element of economic emancipation. Without a measure of economic self-sufficiency it is unlikely that individuals and groups in an age of shrinking public sector resources will ever be truly empowered to transform their dreams and aspirations into reality. If access to information is made difficult, because of the costs to the individual, the capacity to improve one's situation is diminished.

As information becomes commodified and moves from the public sphere – the census, national government statistics – to market research undertaken, bought and sold by private companies, access may increasingly depend on financial resources. The traditional role of the public library – in buying on behalf of the community that which individual members could not personally afford – may be more important than ever with regard to the information that people will need to keep in touch with political, social and economic trends. Given the possible technological scenarios, what is the vocabulary that captures the core ideals and aspirations of our libraries for the twenty-first century? What could a rallying cry for libraries be? "The right to know", a democratic right within many political traditions, may well become the watchword of the public library service. The access to information that libraries provide can be restated as a right – the individual's *right to know* – and the library is perhaps the central public institution to deliver the means to do so. This is a powerful argument, and is already being canvassed by the Council of Europe as a new human right.

The knowledge economy

Information and knowledge are now the equivalent of capital. This idea is a truly paradigmatic shift – the implications of which our society has not yet fully absorbed. It is similar in importance to the shift from the feudal economy based on barter and political patronage to the mercantile economy based on money exchange. Knowledge as the key source of power and wealth focuses our attention sharply on the need to control and have access to information sources in whatever form they may be.

Information now has a clear monetary value. Trading in information is like trading in gold. Under feudalism, power over traditional resources was buttressed and controlled by a panoply of privileges. These included the right of individuals to participate in a trade or guild only after extensive apprenticeships and examinations; or the monopoly rights to trade given to specific persons by those in power. Under mercantilism and later fully blown capitalism these privileges were eroded and a market based on principles of free exchange and the power of finance was established. In the information and "know-how" economy, by contrast, the overriding power of finance is in turn challenged. The capacity of firms or institutions to have access to knowledge may now be as important as access to finance.

PART 2

Institutions in crisis

CHAPTER 3

The end of enlightenment

This book is not about public libraries *per se*, but about what public libraries represent – perhaps one of the greatest educational, cultural and social resources in Britain, admired and emulated throughout the world. It would probably be impossible to invent or construct such a network again. But can it survive and flourish in an era of public service restructuring, economic deregulation, the commercialization of information and the growth of home-based leisure, and other impacts resulting from the wider social transformations that now prevail throughout the world?

For all societies – but particularly "developed" societies – are living through enormous social, political and cultural changes of a kind not experienced since the turbulent and troubled ruptures of industrialization. Post-industrial society is producing patterns of life and lifestyles in the 1990s that are as different to the ordered world of welfarist social democracy of the 1950s as the life of the early industrial slums was to the peasant villages of the generation before. Throughout this book we outline these great demographic and cultural shifts, but here we ask if the public library – which had its origins in the political and educational demands thrown up by that first great transforming period – can survive a second upheaval? Is it essentially an institution of the past, or one that may represent hope for the future?

The public library was quintessentially a product of the age of Enlightenment – its archetypal institution in many ways. Alistair Black and David Muddiman have shown that the development of the public library service was at the heart of the emergence of ethical social policy in Britain, based on Enlightenment principles.[1] The early public libraries were often bitterly contested, but gradually became central to many different, and even opposing, political philosophies of the nineteenth century. The Utilitarian tradition, articulated in part by John Stuart Mill, made a case for the state to provide an environment that would produce the greatest good for the greatest number. The argument that state money spent on public libraries was money saved on gaols and workhouses became, Black and Muddiman argue, a cliché of the public library movement. For the economic liberals, libraries were part of the case for rational recreation advocated as a way of offsetting the debilitating effects of rigid and specialized industrial processes and therefore ultimately a means of enhancing industrial productivity. The nineteenth-century idealist philosophy was also applied to the public library movement. Libraries were places that could offer opportunities for individuals to realize their individual potential. For the mechanics institutes, Chartist groups and other working-class organizations, public libraries extended opportunities for social improvement and political progress. Social reformers saw in the library a place for a new social consensus: a place that symbolized the reduction in inequalities and class conflict. The public library has been a primary institution of this period of history. It found a niche and was able to adapt to the shifting constellation of concerns over education, recreation, economic and social order. The history of the public library movement is a history of nineteenth-century political and ethical philosophy drawn from the tradition of Enlightenment. Can the public library system, which has been so resilient and embedded in the traditions of recent history, adapt once more and embrace the more fundamental challenges to the legacy of Enlightenment now being made?

For the principal belief of that heady era in European thought was that reason, aided and amplified by education, would eventually overcome all, and that a new world order of rational behaviour, civilized institutions, social and political harmony would in time prevail. This project was universal in its aspirations, and transcendental in its philosophy of a greater good that in time would reveal itself through rational thought. Man – and it always was man – finally free from outdated beliefs and superstitions, from material want, would increasingly dwell in the life of the mind which, since Descartes, was to be regarded as a separate and higher sphere of human possibility. The gradual extension of education, of representative democracy, of civil rights, would culminate in an ordered world of peace and stability. That project, that great aspiration, now seems in ruins.

Towards inclusiveness

The "enlightenment project" was undermined from without and within. Darwin's theory of evolution was the first great blow from without, conclusively demonstrating humankind's animal origins, impulses and biological determinisms. Freud's assertion that beneath the calm human exterior lurked deep, violent, irrational feelings and impulses was another great assault on the world of Cartesian logic and Kantian moral autonomy. But already, the failure of the Enlightenment discourse to include women as sovereign subjects and to regard non-European peoples as being included in the realm of significant persons made it in retrospect a bounded, exclusive and excluding project in all kinds of ways.

Philosophically, there has been a revival of older, more naturalist explanations of human behaviour. The American philosopher Annette Baier has recently described how women, for example, find it easier to adopt "a naturalist view of persons, like Hume's or Darwin's or Freud's, that takes our biological nature seriously, takes it not as a handicap but as a source of strengths as well as weaknesses".[2] Richard Rorty has also drawn a clear distinction between "a Kantian, non-naturalistic view of persons with a Humean naturalistic view – contrasting moral psychologies which emphasise autonomy and rationality with those which emphasise interdependence and benevolence".[3] Much recent scientific work in biology, genetics, psychology and natural history, with its references to blind watchmakers, selfish genes and so on, has reminded us that we remain closer to nature than our enlightened forebears hoped or thought we would.

Non-Western traditions

But there have been many other challenges to the Enlightenment view. The global history of imperialism, colonialism, and its counter-movements and struggles has brought new attitudes and relationships between nations and cultures, particularly around questions as to the beneficial effects of "enlightened" European domination and control, first spatial and increasingly economic. Educational theorists are beginning to argue that the Western bias for logical thinking based on rationality has denied the potential of other kinds of human intelligences.[4] The despoliation of large parts of the earth in the name of world trade, the disruption and sometimes extinction of indigenous cultures and lifestyles, which in retrospect were more ecological and benign than their "enlightened" successors, have posed a serious challenge to the "scientific" and "economic" rationality of the West. Partly as a result of these great connecting and now disconnecting empires, enormous migrations of people are now a feature of all continents, nations, states and cities, and when people move they take with them not just belongings but also different religious and philosophical beliefs, cultural attitudes and lifestyles, which are not easily shed – or erased. Many towns and cities in Britain now have significant ethnic minority communities, bringing different customs, languages, cuisines; alongside many Anglican churches, Methodist chapels or Catholic churches, are now to be found Hindu temples, Muslim mosques and other buildings representing different spiritual values or faiths. Urban cosmopolitanism throughout the world is now increasingly likely to be the norm rather than the exception.

Representation and social democracy

In economic and political terms, the achievements have also only been partial, and remain stubbornly incomplete. Standards of living have incrementally risen in the West, although increasingly unequally with the decline of social democracy, and while some former Third World countries are now experiencing tremendous growth, others, notably in Africa, are experiencing increased poverty and immiseration. Hence the large-scale population movements from the poorer countries to the richer ones. Representative parliamentary democracy, the political means for achieving the ideals of rational, civil society, is now increasingly distrusted: for many it remains a cover for old-fashioned privilege and vested interests, as in Britain it has signally failed to represent women's interests, the views of ethnic minorities, the longer-term political issues of ecology and sustainability, and is regarded as centralist, metropolitan and dominated by business interests, and consequently held in lowering national esteem.

New forms of democracy – proportional representation, strengthening regional and local government, greater use of referenda – are now urged

22

from all quarters, in order to "represent" those whom representative democracy continually seems to fail. The nation state is losing its cohesive power, as specifically European political and legal powers grow stronger, and global consumer identities erode traditional loyalties to place and flag. The project of finding applications for, and making sense of, the possibilities offered by the new communications technologies is underway. Class identities are being partially replaced by consumer lifestyles; inherited gender roles and obligations are slowly being replaced by relationships and familial patterns freely entered into and based on choice. Economic individualism – "there is no such thing as society" – wreaks havoc in communities traditionally based on collectivist identities and forms of civil life based on trust.

It is these great economic, political, geographical and cultural shifts that have produced the questions raised by "post-modernist" philosophy, most notably whether the project of "universalism" is now at an end, and that what we are witnessing and living through is a shift back to a world of differences, a plurality of separate – though sometimes overlapping – communities and cultural identities. The grand narrative of universal reason, of human enlightenment, of everybody eventually becoming citizens of an ordered and rational world now seems chimerical, leading to the question that if the Enlightenment has failed have its institutions failed too? This, today, we believe to be the problem of problems: reconciling shared values, the "common interest", with those of cultural difference and diversity. And nowhere is this issue more germane and pressing than in the consideration of how – and if – the public library will survive and adapt to serve the needs and interests of future generations.

The general interest

It is the argument of this book that the public library is in a uniquely strong position to meet and address these issues and, in doing so, possibly show the way to a new political rapprochement or cultural "settlement". For the library has grown to embody both universal values as well as those of distinct communities, in much the same way that it has successfully dissolved the traditional antinomies of "public" and "private", "individual" and "collective", key themes of this book and dealt with later in much greater depth. It has always been – in theory and more importantly in practice – an inclusive organization. It welcomes everybody without imposing rules or entry criteria. With its reference books, its networked access to published material of all kinds, it represents the inherited culture of rational thought, self-education and individual enlightenment. It has sustained an enviable tradition – unlike many other institutions – of non-sectarianism and secularism, and librarians are widely perceived to be non-judgemental and tolerant to all opinion. Because it is a voluntary institution it has never attempted to impose set ideas or asserted its values above those of its users.

Yet it has also represented a strong tradition of responsiveness to local distinctiveness and local cultural identities. It is both a general provider and a specialist provider, for the system has developed a tradition of specialist collections, adopted by different local services, but accessible to all through the inter-library loan scheme. Thus, an inner London branch library may not only hold a general collection of reference books, encyclopaedias (the European Enlightenment was associated with the French *encyclopaedists*), novels for lending, CDs and cassettes, but also house a specialist collection of Polish literature, or Afro-Caribbean literature, or HIV and AIDS materials, or West African music, or Jewish folk music. (In fact all of these specialist collections are offered by public libraries within the space of 2 square miles in inner London – diversity is something libraries know very well.)[5]

It could be argued that diversity itself is predicated on some agreed general interests and universal rights. The right to know is one shared by all communities and cultures in developing societies, particularly where economic and social power is increasingly based on knowledge, and yet the project of inventing a role for communications technology as an integral part of the public library service has only just begun. Those denied knowledge quickly become economically disfranchised. The right to paid employment or the means of livelihood is again back on the political agenda as people realize that unemployment is not only an economic issue but a social issue with enormous damaging and corrosive power. Without the means to economic wherewithal, cultural diversity is simply an assertion rather than an achieved and fulfilled condition. The environment also represents a general interest over and above the interests of specific individuals or communities. In short, society is going to have to find ways of accommodating both general and particular interests, both collective and individual rights and responsibilities, both universal and culturally specific aspirations and forms of belonging, both local and global awareness of place and identity.

All of these issues are played out in the first instance locally. And diversity in itself is not enough. As Paul Hoggett has noted in his study of associational life – the rich life of voluntary organizations, mutual aid societies, community groups and associations, whether based on ethnic minority identity, gender, sexual identity or whatever – in Britain, there are disadvantages to unalloyed diversity.

> One of the great disadvantages of the associational sphere resides in its tendency towards particularism. If this is to be checked as the associational sphere grows in importance then it is vital that strong local institutions exist that can represent the "general good" in counterposition to the "particular goods" engendered within the associational sphere. The quality of local democracy depends upon the existence both of strong civic associations and strong representative institutions. Otherwise the shift towards more pluralistic forms simply encourages the further fragmentation of civil society, particularly if such associations are being deliberately drawn into competition for scarce public resources.[6]

Arguments about appropriate organizational forms for various kinds of services are now high on the political agenda.

CHAPTER 4

The changing role of public institutions

In the past decade, developed and developing societies throughout the world have witnessed a struggle between public (state) and private (commercial) attempts to provide the framework for economic, social and cultural development. As the state bureaucracies (and gerontocracies) of communism have imploded, so the arguments for allowing the market to play the leading role in development have gained the edge in political thinking in many parts of the world. Britain, taking its lead from the Chicago school of Friedmanite monetarism, in turn has carried the flag for allowing the market to set the pace of future economic and political change. Privatization of state assets has been pioneered in Britain and emulated widely in other countries. Even so, public expenditure as a percentage of the Gross National Product (GNP) continues to rise in Britain, and notions of the "lean state", the "enabling state" or of the "minimal state", although widely espoused, seem no nearer to fruition than they were when such ideas first gained ascendancy.

A "market-led" approach to public provision has already affected many public cultural institutions, largely through the requirement on local authorities to put out to tender many services and facilities that were traditionally provided direct. Compulsory Competitive Tendering (CCT) now applies in many ways to local authority leisure provision: theatres have been handed over on management contracts to private leisure companies, or set up as trusts; swimming pools and sports centres have likewise been partly or wholly put out to private management; catering in many public institutions has been franchised out, and facilities have been handed over to community groups or groups of

26

volunteers. Increasingly, local authority provision has been put on a client–contractor basis, with the local authority drawing up a specification for services that in turn its own in-house team agree to run, or may well be put out to tender. All these changes affect libraries. Some technical work is now routinely put out to tender and handled by commercial companies – book lamination and processing, for example, or cleaning. Increasingly, new services, or what are regarded as "non-core" services, such as video lending or business information, are established on a "self-funding" basis only. All of these gradual shifts bring into question the very nature of "public" forms of provision, which, as is argued below, has frequently been associated with "free" or "subsidized". Politics and economics always go hand in hand. Now it is already possible to contemplate the situation whereby one local authority prepares the brief for running its library service, only to have a rival local authority successfully bid to win the contract and run its services. Where do local identity and local distinctiveness fit then?

The economic case for market provision with regard to libraries has been most graphically put by the Adam Smith Institute in a briefing paper published in 1986, when it argued that since it then cost £1.24 to issue each book (a crude figure calculated by dividing the total cost of public library services by the number of books issued, as if libraries did nothing else), then libraries should be closed and the books given away free in the street – a cheaper solution.[1] This is the market-based approach *in extremis*, and because of that it illustrates all the issues around public cultural provision in graphic detail. For it is a wholly reductionist argument that defines libraries simply in terms of one activity – lending books. It excludes all the unquantifiable factors in the service, such as browsing, information enquiries, a place to meet or study, a social venue and so on. In short, the argument here is about defining what is uniquely special about public cultural institutions, which, while they may benefit from varying degrees of developing a mixed economy, cannot wholly be reduced to a producer–consumer cash nexus.

What is a public cultural institution?

The essential ethos of the public library and other public cultural institutions such as museums or galleries derives from the tautological fact that they are indeed public. They are not like the private library of a gentlemen's club or an educational institution that requires qualifications to join, or a commercial library. They are open to anyone.

This seems a very simple and admirable principle. Underlying it, however, is a complex history and a set of ideas about what makes societies work. These ideas, which together form the tradition of public goods and values, civic virtues and ideals, are arguably in greater difficulty today than they have ever been: their exponents find it hard to explain why inclusiveness is so much better than exclusivity, or why public provision remains legitimate when many people are meeting their needs for culture or information in the private sector. After all, in the modern world many people buy their own transport systems, buy their own houses, increasingly buy their own health care, so why not buy their own culture?

The definition of what "public" now means is varied and contested, and the use in cultural debates somewhat vague and unclear. At times this lack of clarity has benefited the professions in cultural institutions, as the term "public" exudes a certain "goodness". With the notion of the "idea of the public" itself under attack over the last decade there is a need for reinterpretation, and it is important to make assumptions clear. The idea of the "public" veers between meaning "concerning the people as a whole", "open to all", "maintained at the expense of the community" or simply "serving the community". On the other hand, it can be argued that one of the most important functions that the library fulfils – unknowingly – is actually to create the "public" as a recognizable constituency.

An epoch of institutional upheaval

For many public institutions the 1980s and 1990s are likely, in retrospect, to prove as epochal as the 1840s and 1850s, when many of them were founded. The mid-nineteenth century saw a welter of public institution building and regulation – from the Municipal Corporations Act of 1835, the Ten Hours Act of 1847 governing working hours, the Public Health Act of 1848 creating local Boards of Health, and the Museums Act of 1845, to the Public Libraries Act of 1850, which (together with the Education Act of 1870) created many of the structures and institutions that have survived, only slightly amended, until today. They were created in an era of rationalism and growth, and in an idealistic vision of the benign and ever-powerful role of the state in moderating and governing public life. Today the powerful state, or indeed local authority, is regarded with suspicion, as paternalistic, interfering, often putting the interests of the institutions and the people that run them above the interests of the people they are supposed to serve. Consumer-sovereignty has been reasserted, and *the purposes of the public institutions of the twenty-first century have thus to be re-evaluated.*

Universal provision, redistribution and social justice

The public library has been informed from the beginning with the principle of free public access. In many ways this was the precursor to the establishment of free state education in 1870, and the free National Health Service (NHS) from 1945, commonly known as the principle of "universal provision". Free access to all was part of the programme of a more equitable society in which what were seen as essentially rights – knowledge, education, health – would not only be made available to those who could afford them, but to everybody, and paid for out of general taxation. It was assumed that over time free access would lead to a widening of opportunity and a breaking-down of previous inequalities of wealth, status and power.

In fact what happened, it can be argued, was the reverse. The principle of universal, non-means-tested provision has *in practice unduly benefited the middle class rather than the working class,* even while providing a general safety net for everybody. This first became evident in the 1960s when sociologists looked at the relationship between social class and educational opportunity in Britain and were dismayed to find that working-class representation at university level had scarcely altered in the forty years since the 1920s. The Black Report on the NHS found a similar pattern: that although everybody paid taxes to fund a free health service, by far the most uses of it, and benefits derived from it, were taken up by the more demanding and more articulate middle class.[2] It could be argued that the public library service is in the same mould. Funded by universal taxation, it is more used by the already educated than by those at the bottom of the social scale.

This has certainly been the Achilles' heel of redistributive social democracy: that, in short, universal free provision doesn't always redress inequalities but sometimes exacerbates them. The "consumer-pays" model of the thorough-going market place seems to redress the balance in favour of the principle that if you don't use it then you don't have to pay for it.

A genuine public good

But the story doesn't end there. For while free, universal provision is deeply imperfect, it does still offer opportunities (and the all-important safety net) that a market-based system might not. Some, perhaps many, working-class children did get to university; some working-class people's lives have been saved by expensive NHS treatment; many people who use the library because it is free would not do so if they had to pay. In the end a free service does keep lots of doors open, even if it only signposts them in places and ways that favour the already well-educated middle classes. It also is there for those who may never use it – but who might. It is probably a very good thing not to have to go into hospital or spend a lifetime on expensive drugs, but does this mean that one shouldn't pay a contribution for the availability of this service if one suddenly did become very ill. *It is not use but the availability for use* that most strongly characterizes universal, tax-paid forms of provision such as health care, the provision of parks, libraries, public road systems, and other elements of the social and economic infrastructure that underpins society.

A wholly charged-for system of cultural provision – such as the opera house, the theatre, the concert hall (even though they are also subsidized from taxes) – often ends up with a narrow, coterie audience, who know what they like and like what they know. There is no room for people to try it once and see if they like it, which free access always offers and sometimes succeeds in providing. It is perhaps for this reason that the public library is *the* popular cultural institution, while most of the others are not. Yet if the principle of free access is to be retained, then the library world will have to be better equipped at demonstrating that it is a genuine public good, that its services do reach some of the most disadvantaged sections of the community that a charged-for service would not, and that it is not an instrument by which cultural resources are paid for out of the public purse for the benefit of a minority who are already economically and culturally privileged.

The changing role of the public library

We live, therefore, in an era of institutional upheaval: "all that is solid melts in the air". Not only have the hard and fast boundaries between the "public" and the "private" sectors loosened up, but other transforming changes are in play. Many "modernized" facilities and institutions now combine what were traditionally separate functions and activities, particularly in retailing and service industries: the grocery shop sells stamps and offers a photocopying service; libraries sell books, theatre tickets and travelcards; Marks & Spencer has moved into publishing and banking; the BBC is now a global record producer and publisher; Waterstones organize poetry readings; McDonalds now provide newspapers for their customers as the nineteenth-century coffee houses once did; ethnic minority grocery shops sell videos; libraries open coffee bars; the high street bank is disappearing in favour of telephone banking and cash from a machine; the garden centre replaces the seaside as the destination for a Sunday outing in the car. People watch TV in order to get a degree, and tune into the radio for medical advice. Into this febrile world of institutional disintegration and reformation, the library service has found itself fully stretched and overextended, despite a very resilient tradition of responsiveness to cultural change.

Key moments

Over time, the public library service has naturally evolved, responding to new needs and interests in the wider society. Historians of the service have broadly observed the following periods of development and policy changes of the public library movement:

- The founding era from the 1850s to the end of the nineteenth century, when the public library was regarded as a key instrument of working-class literacy and self-education. Growing out of the mechanics institutes in some places, out of the teetotal movement in others, the library was regarded as an alternative to the pub, but also – by the social reformers – as an alternative to violent social unrest and political upheaval. Social change, it was argued, would come through education and enlightenment. This formative period was obviously marked by the realization that borrowing rather than buying was a more effective way of providing people with books they could either not afford to buy, or didn't want to buy and keep; the public library was in many ways modelled on the commercial subscription or "circulating" libraries. As with the subscription libraries, the new local authority libraries "created" a public for the books they lent and promoted.

- The development of the County library service following the Public Libraries Act of 1919 marked another watershed. This established a strong suburban and rural usership for libraries (and a middle-class readership as well) which in turn created a reading public for the "middlebrow" romance, country house detective story and other elements of what became staple library fare. Publishers began to take a keen interest in this new market, as did writers. The buying power of libraries became a new cultural force in literature. Yet in spite of these developments, until the Second World War the library was still essentially justified in educational terms as part of the self-improvement paradigm.

- The post-war boom in library building was part of the social democratic settlement, along with health centres, new schools and other building blocks of the "universal" welfare state. The historian Raphael Samuel has described some of London's post-war libraries (such as the one in Finsbury) as "avatars of democratic modernism", promoting film shows, lending records, and in other ways espousing a "modernist" cultural trajectory.[3] Nevertheless, some argue that from the post-war period onwards the library was beginning to come under threat from other institutions, especially through the massive investment in education, and began to lose its core rationale.

- The 1960s' "renaissance" in British children's literature, and the renewed interest in children's reading, owes much to the efforts of children's librarians to engage with publishers and writers over questions of gender, race and class images in children's books. They encouraged writers to be more imaginative in their work, to reflect the multicultural society Britain was becoming, often inviting writers into libraries to meet and talk with their young readers. The growing close relationship between children's librarians, publishers and writers had an enormously beneficial effect on children's literature, which continues to this day. Recent initiatives around book promotion schemes and projects in public libraries suggest that the situation for adult fiction is now similarly being redressed.

- The rediscovery of the issue of adult literacy in the 1970s. (June 1993 estimates assume a UK population of people lacking functional literacy at 6 million.) An increasing number of people with a low level of functional literacy produced a new role for libraries. Nowadays computer and visual literacy are increasingly significant as life skills, and the library will have to address these issues if it wants to remain centre stage.
- The development of "community librarianship" in the 1970s. This reflected a need to make the public library more relevant to people in disadvantaged communities, for whom welfare rights information, basic literacy and numeracy texts, or a community group meeting place might be as important as the traditional book stock. Out of this new orientation to community need has grown the recent development in public libraries of resources and facilities for "open learning".
- The impact of the 1974 local government reorganization and the move of library services often into new education or leisure directorates with a wider remit than libraries alone.
- The growing impact of new technology in the 1980s and 1990s. First, as an aid to the "behind the desk" service – cataloguing, searching, issuing – but increasingly as part of the library repertoire: view data, CD-ROM, microfiche, interactive open learning materials.
- The contemporary "crisis" exemplified in current concerns with local government reorganization, CCT, a greater range of charged-for services, the possible development of some libraries being run as independent trusts, a greater differentiation between the "leisure library", the "business library", the "open learning library" and/or the "community library". The epoch of "reinventing government" and the rise of "third sector" institutions.

Many may observe that in the recent promotion of the public library as a community educational resource, the wheel has come full circle. The development of open learning facilities in libraries is in a sense a return to the original values and philosophy that established the public library system 150 years before. For while we can see that the library ethos has undergone many changes since its inception, there are certain elements that have remained fundamental.

A comprehensive service

Since 1964, local authorities have had a statutory obligation to provide "a comprehensive and efficient" library service. In practice, libraries, like other institutions in an era of upheaval, have been taking on new functions that seem to have nothing to do with their basic service, and at the same time discarding others. The most common activities that those surveyed claim to use the library for, according to a MORI survey conducted in 1991, include:

- adult book lending (65%)
- children's book lending (65%)
- reference library (30%)
- seeking advice or help from staff (30%)
- looking up local community information/leaflets (27%)
- photocopying (15%)
- reading newspapers/magazines (13%)
- record and CD lending (12%)
- video lending or hire (12%)
- looking up something on computer or card index (12%)
- inter-library loans (11%)
- public meetings (2%).[4]

There are, however, a whole series of other activities that take place in libraries, sometimes in over half of the libraries we surveyed, which significantly were not covered in the MORI survey. They include activities that are seen to present some of the library's more "intangible" benefits, such as:

- using the library as an exhibition space
- picture-borrowing
- local archives
- answering telephone enquiries
- genealogical services
- multimedia services
- local publishing
- selling books
- selling theatre tickets
- tourist information
- business information
- open learning
- providing on-line work stations

- spaces and tables for doing homework/study
- story-telling
- toy libraries
- playing chess and table games
- providing school holiday programmes.

There are also a series of functions that the library performs that are purely social yet, according to our research, are nevertheless important for users. They include:

- using the café, where available
- meeting people
- social interchange between librarian and "regulars"
- keeping warm
- using the library as an urban haven.

This diversity of functions is not unusual. *The key point is that libraries accommodate many more additional activities than simply lending books.* At what point then can these other or "peripheral" activities so displace "core" activities that the library itself disappears? What are the pressures that are driving libraries continually to extend their scope?

Never able to say no

The last decade has seen enormous changes in education provision, management and delivery. The 1988 Education Act, introducing local management into schools, and the detaching of schools from local authority control have had a major impact on public libraries, as has the rapid expansion of further and higher education in the same period. As Sir Christopher Ball noted in his paper "The learning society", "participation in higher education has risen from 1 in 8 to 1 in 5 between 1979 and 1991 (the target is 1 in 3 by the year 2000)".[5] The implications of these trends are enormous. Public libraries are increasingly servicing many of these new students by providing books, advice and study spaces. Yet the public library service was clearly never consulted about the implications of these policy decisions and has had to respond reactively and by default rather than through strategic choice. This political invisibility of the library is something we will return to in Chapter 6.

A further area where libraries are having to meet a need established by other organizations who may no longer be able to fulfil that function is in welfare rights and citizens advice. Once again the library responds to an agenda set by other organizations and external interests. As funding for the generic agencies has atrophied or is under pressure, libraries, *de facto* if not *de jure*, are picking up the policy responsibility.

There is also a tradition of libraries being used as arts centres. Peggy Heeks's report on *Public libraries and the arts* found that nearly half of Britain's libraries provided accommodation for voluntary groups and over half provided space specially for arts exhibitions.[6] She also found evidence of libraries being used for live music performances, drama performances, writers workshops and other literary activities, for photography projects and the screening of films. The reason for the library accruing these functions was either because the library was regarded as the only available space in a town or because it was seen as the most accessible.

A further example is the way in which the library was significantly affected by the impact of the government's "care in the community" policy. The libraries in all case study areas had to deal with an increased number of homeless users and the mentally ill as part of their daily routine. In the process, the library acquired yet another role that it had not asked for, was not consulted about, didn't have the expertise to execute, and was not funded to fulfil.

The strength but also the problem of the library is that it is *an inclusive organization* allowing anyone who so wishes to enter its doors and "do their own thing". It does not exclude. This makes it vulnerable to exploitation, consciously or unconsciously, by other agencies. In effect *the library has become a service provider of last resort.* This is not necessarily a happy scenario, because it both confuses librarians as to what their own precise role is, and often forces them to undertake tasks for which they are not necessarily equipped or trained. It means that libraries are active in policy areas that are not their own, and without the strategic connections that would make involvement more coherent and effective.

And while all these new responsibilities are accruing to the libraries, they are not receiving extra funds to pay for them and instead are being asked to generate more revenue, be it through charging for traditional services (such as increasing the levels of fines) or by making all new services – such as video loans, selling local publications, photocopying or running a bookshop – self-financing. Part social worker, part information analyst, part commercial entrepreneur, it is no wonder that many librarians are experiencing an identity crisis.

CHAPTER 5

The modern library network

The first public libraries in Britain, as we have noted, were established in the middle of the last century, largely as a result of the 1850 Public Libraries Act, and since then have largely enjoyed continual growth. Library services vary in quantity and quality in different parts of the country, which is not surprising since it is a local service that different political and social traditions value unequally. Some facts may help to explain this.

Numbers

In 1993 there were 2,487 public libraries in the United Kingdom that were open to the public for more than 30 hours per week. Including mobile libraries, there were 4,778 libraries open more than 10 hours a week. This is a slight increase on the figure of 12 years ago. Contrary to the generally accepted image of a declining service, roughly 300 new public libraries were built during the 1980s. In spite of restrictions on capital expenditure by local authorities, major library projects were completed in the London boroughs of Bexley, Hillingdon, Ealing, Haringey, Hounslow and Ilford among others. In Glasgow, the extension to the Mitchell Library was opened in 1981, making it the largest reference library in Europe. In 1988, the biggest public library in Wales was opened in Cardiff. Dorset County Council, one of the case study authorities, has developed 20 new libraries during the last decade.

Libraries have also spread their wings. The number of individual points served by the library service, including hospitals, old people's homes and prisons, has increased from 11,346 in 1982 to 19,095 in 1992. In 1993 there were 709 mobile libraries serving rural or isolated communities. Financial restrictions on local councils have, however, affected opening hours. The number of libraries open for more than 60 hours per week (something like a minimum of 9am–7pm from Monday to Saturday) has reduced from 90 to 48 between 1982 and 1992. Several local authorities have experimented with Sunday opening. The number of people who work in libraries has reduced from a peak of 29,911 in 1987 to 28,259 in 1992. Of these, 7,651 were professionally trained and 18,859 were library assistants.[1]

Costs

In 1991–2 every person in the United Kingdom paid on average £12.94 per annum for the service, whether they used it or not. This figure has risen in real terms from £11.35 in 1981, an increase of 14.01%. In 1994, in comparison, the BBC licence fee was £80 per annum, car road tax £120, telephone rental about £80, and a subscription to a weekly magazine about £80. A single CD cost about £12 to buy and the average hardback book £16. The total figure for running the library service, whether from central or local government sources, stood at £746 million in 1991–2. This compares with £639 million at constant prices ten years before, and represents an increase in real terms of 16.7%.

The general public is rarely aware of how much new library buildings cost or indeed of the costs of similar services such as sports centres, museums or arts centres. By way of example we outline in very general terms some typical library costs. These figures are intended as guidelines only. The specific circumstances of new library buildings can significantly alter the capital costs.

For a *small library* intended to serve a small community of between 5,000 and 8,000 people, an all-inclusive cost would be around £300,000. This would include between £150,000 and £200,000 for a new building of about 180 square metres and £30,000–£60,000 for fittings, a stock of about 11,000 and the cost of professional fees. Staffing would typically be around 2.5 people and annual overheads in the order of £40,000.

A *mobile library* equipped with approximately 3,000 books costs in the order of £50,000 to buy and fit out, with annual overheads of about £25,000.

A *medium-sized new library* serving a population base of around 60,000–80,000 and with 1,500 square metres of floor space costs in the order of £1,700,000. Such a library is likely to be a replacement and although it would stock between 70,000 and 80,000 titles, most of these books would have been transferred from the old location. Staffing would typically be around 12 full-time equivalents with annual overheads running in the order of £210,000.

A new *larger central library* with a floor area of 2,500 square metres serving a population in the region of 150,000 or more inhabitants would cost in the order of £4,500,000–£5,000,000. It would stock around 110,000 titles, most of which would have been transferred, and have annual overheads running at £400,000 plus.[2]

Book issues and other services

Libraries are not just used for the borrowing of books. But book issues still play a central role in the service that libraries offer, and often supply the statistics by which libraries are judged. The issuing of books has in fact declined from 660.31 million in 1980–1 to 560.83 million in 1990–91, a decrease of 15% over ten years. Nevertheless, 1.6 million books are borrowed each day from UK public libraries. The figures for 1991–2 show an upturn in issues to 580 million. Books still account for 92% of the libraries' spending on materials, and 64 out of 167 library authorities still do not spend any money on videos, although practically all purchase audio materials. A relatively small 5% of total borrowings are for records, CDs, cassettes and videos, suggesting that the fears of some that books are being wholly displaced by CDs and videos are somewhat premature.[3]

As far as the types of books borrowed are concerned, trends show that junior non-fiction, literature, religion and sociology have all markedly increased in popularity between 1985 and 1990, while westerns, romances, humour and war have all shown decreases.

Therefore, one must conclude that overall the library network has expanded, but the majority of service points are open only between 30 and 44 hours per week. Since core opening hours tend to match the 9am–5pm working day, the library service – despite having expanded – runs a serious risk of excluding an important audience of working people. The issue of opening hours is likely to become more important in the light of social and demographic changes that are altering the pattern of people's daily lives and their expectations of services and facilities.

Who uses public libraries?

It is claimed that 58% of the population hold a library card. However, surveys of actual use (MORI 1992, Book Marketing Limited (BML) 1992) would indicate that around 30% of the population are active library users, with an additional 28% occasional users. Library users are also bookshop users. The BML research shows that those inclined to buy books are also likely to borrow them from libraries.[3]

The public library is one of the most popular cultural facilities in Britain today. The library audience as a whole has a wider social base and the public library is more successful than other cultural institutions in attracting use across social class. The BML 1992 research showed that all social groups are well represented in library use statistics (see Table 5.1).

The question of the relationship between social class and library usage is extraordinarily complex, and cannot be reduced to a simple assertion either that "libraries are used predominantly by the middle class" or that "libraries are for those who cannot afford to use bookshops or pay for advice". First, it is more accurate to say that libraries in general reflect

Table 5.1   Social class and library use.

Social class	% of UK population	% of library users
AB	15	19
C1	23	27
C2	29	27
DE	33	27

Source: BML 1992 survey. Table 3, p. 21.

and respond to the social demographics of the district in which they are located – a truism perhaps, but nevertheless important to reassert. Unlike other cultural institutions – theatres, arts centres, opera houses, and so on – the library service is probably as strong in working-class areas as it is in middle- or upper-class areas. It is a genuinely distributed cultural service. Secondly, rather than simply reflect and respond to the nuances of class patterns of behaviour and mobility, *libraries have often been a cause of social mobility*. The use of the public library has enabled people to take the route of social mobility. And at different times in their lives, people of different classes fall in and out of patterns of library usage that cannot be simply defined as a fixed socio-economic causal relationship. The entrepreneurial merchant banker may never go near a library in the course of his hectic and dynamic business life, but if and when overnight he is asked to clear his desk, he may well be at the doors of the public library the following week, looking either for careers advice or some relaxing reading. Many working people are too busy to use libraries, but when retirement comes they fall back into the pattern of their childhood, calling in at the library regularly for something new to read. There are no iron laws of use and non-use, and few patterns of uninterrupted continuity.

Age and gender

Usage by the under-20s and over-60s is somewhat higher than average: 29% of all regular borrowers are over 65, although this age group makes up only 19% of the population; 59% of library users are women and 41% are men (BML 1992). Other above average users are students and the unemployed. A recent survey by the London borough of Hounslow showed a close match between the age profile of library users and that of the borough population as a whole. Even so, the 60+ group was 6% higher in the library users' profile than in the borough population, and the 25–34-year-olds were under-represented in the library users' profile compared to the borough profile by 5%. Research recently carried out in Birmingham on library use by elderly people concluded that a very high proportion of elderly people in the city benefit from the library service.[5]

Recent research by MORI for the Audit Commission found that a significant factor affecting library use was the presence of children in the household: 71% of respondents with children (aged between 9 and 14) used the library, compared with the overall figure of 58%.[6]

User research

Many library authorities carry out regular reviews of library use. However, these tend to follow slightly different formats from authority to authority and are thus difficult to compare and contrast. Typically they explore age, gender and frequency of use. Our research interviews revealed that many library managers are concerned about non-use of libraries. Some authorities have begun to investigate the reasons why people choose not to use libraries. However, the concern about non-use is often predicated on a sense that the library or staff have failed to convince non-users of their need for library services. There is a case for more systematic research into library use and non-use that can inform the future development of the library.

One concern in analyzing the statistics is that evidence is beginning to show that some young people in some areas have a poor view of libraries. They consider libraries to be old-fashioned, or not of a high enough quality. These are the people who tend to be interested in new technology and new ways of finding information, a target group that the public library of the future cannot afford to ignore.

CHAPTER 6

Political invisibility

Yet despite the pervasive influence that the public library service plays in many people's lives, and in the social fabric of the places in which they live, the service itself is the subject of the seemingly contradictory values of high public esteem and low political visibility and concern. "Dying in a welter of goodwill" was the phrase used in the original Comedia report, although as that report also showed, in many places the library service was still thriving. Nevertheless, on the national political stage – in parliament, in the committee rooms and lobbying parlours, in the editorials of the national press, in broadcasting and elsewhere – public libraries remain a subject of, at most, mild interest and occasional comic repartee. When the Comedia report was published, the editor of one national heavyweight newspaper declined to carry any article or feature about the report because, he baldly stated, "nobody's interested in libraries". Yet how does one square this apparent national political indifference – the local situation is often quite different – with the ministerial statement by Richard Luce MP in the Introduction to the government's 1988 Green Paper *Financing our public library service*, that "I believe that we have in Britain the finest public library service in the world." A world-class service admired and emulated throughout the world but ignored at home? Such political invisibility deserves wider consideration.

The London effect

A starting point for any understanding of the low political clout of the public library service has to be a consideration of what might be termed "the London effect". As was noted above on the national press response to the Comedia report, London journalists and commentators often have a very jaundiced view of the public library service, comparing the present crisis-ridden state of many inner London borough services with a halcyon memory of the benign provincial library service of their child-hoods. There is some objective evidence to support this public sense that libraries in London are less valued and appreciated than libraries else-where in the country, and those in inner London even less appreciated than those in outer London.

The public library service also suffers from an unusual reversal of cul-tural influence compared with most other cultural facilities, in that it is weakest at the centre and strongest at the periphery, in terms of the national cultural geography. It is a genuinely successful decentralized cultural institution. Excluding the British Library – which is not a public library – many of the finest public libraries are to be found in the great provincial cities rather than in London. This of course is quite the oppo-site to the case with regard to opera houses, theatres, concert halls, museums and virtually all other cultural venues, where the London facilities seem to represent the most prestigious and highly funded of these otherwise nationally distributed cultural forms. Many of them are gilded additionally with the Royal seal: the Royal Opera House, the Royal National Theatre, the Royal Academy, the Royal Ballet, the Royal Philharmonic Orchestra and so on. To be on the Board of any of these powerful "national" institutions is to have "arrived" at the centre of cultural influence and power. Unhappily, this is not the case with the public library service. Another paradox: literature is said to be Britain's strongest cultural tradition, publishing one of its most internationally prodigious cultural industries, and library usage the most popular cul-tural activity of all, yet in some ways it is the very democracy of public library usage that militates against its national prestige.

One obvious reason for the fact that libraries are the exception to the rule – that London provision dominates all cultural institutions – is that the public library service is essentially a local service, managed and delivered locally. It is a network of cultural distribution rather than of cultural production. All books are the same whether they are borrowed and read in Barrow rather than Bayswater, Kingswinford rather than Knightsbridge. This is not the same with live performances of *King Lear* or Elgar's "In the South", for example, where the London production is likely to be a heavily subsidized professional production rather than a local amateur one. However, there are other reasons that go towards explaining the public library's national political invisibility, apart from its quintessentially local character.

Political neutrality

Significant among these other factors is the long-standing tradition of the political neutrality of the professional librarian. Because of the almost unique aura that surrounds books – dealt with in the section on the "libraryness" of libraries – regarding issues of freedom of thought and fears of censorship among others, librarians have guarded and valued their political neutrality in all aspects, seeking to provide for all shades of political opinion in their book selection procedures, and fending off interventions by local party politicians to "reflect" the interests and political values of the incumbent local council, whatever party that may be. This has been an admirable tradition, despite real issues and controversies over questions of racism and sexism in children's books in recent years. Nevertheless, political neutrality at a local level may be one (very good) thing, but political self-effacement on the national stage is potentially disastrous. For while public librarians hope that their services shine like a good deed in a naughty world, the fund-raisers, marketing managers, sponsorship agents, trustees and board members of the theatres, museums, concert halls and opera houses are fighting their case every inch of the way in the corridors of power, canapés in one hand, spreadsheets and three-year business plans in the other. Boardroom battles at the Royal Opera House are front page news, as are sponsorship deals for the RSC; yet these are cultural institutions that largely serve a metropolitan minority elite.

In the course of the Comedia study, a press cuttings service was enlisted to provide details of all national coverage of public library issues from June 1992 to June 1993. Such coverage as there was was almost exclusively devoted to financial "cuts", closures and reductions in opening hours, CCT and the parlous state of the school library service.

45

Libraries are reported at a technical/service level rather than as a central cultural institution of our times. For example, the book pages of most national newspapers, some of which even have separate book review supplements, rarely discuss public libraries, or indeed regard the views of librarians as relevant to the literary issues of the day. Yet, as many people will borrow the reviewed books from the public library as will buy them.

Arguing the case

It can be argued that librarians have confused party political neutrality with intellectual neutrality, and have wrongly eschewed literary and cultural judgements of their own. It has been pointed out that librarians are rarely invited to provide literary opinions in the book pages or on television, nor are they invited to become judges of literary prizes or in a number of other ways take part in literary and critical debate. No public librarian has been a Booker Prize judge as far as is known. Regarding themselves often as having primarily technical skills – in cataloguing, accessing information systems and databases, managing effective book, record and video lending systems – the wider world has come to regard them as having only these skills, and as having nothing valid to say in literary and cultural matters.

This situation is not the case with the world of children's librarianship, where certainly since the 1960s, children's librarians have played a significant and valuable role in encouraging debate about the quality of children's writing and book illustration, in being regarded by publishers as significant intellectual presences in the field, and in giving their opinions and judgements that are are regarded as valid in book reviewing and prize-giving.

Widening the debate

It is significant that the Comedia report was possibly the first *independent* review of the public library service in Britain for more than fifty years. As one of Britain's most stable and resilient cultural institutions, the public library has avoided controversy, and quietly got on with its own work. While there is certainly much in-house research about public libraries, several professional journals, a powerful and respected professional organization (the Library Association), debate is very much a closed and internal affair. Librarians do not make news, nor do they tend to get involved in other people's affairs – education, social policy, telecommunications policy and so on. There has been little national strategic thinking, and the public library service has been housed and monitored since the war in the Department of Education and Science (where it was almost certainly overshadowed by education), in the Office of Arts and Libraries (where the Arts Council made all the political running), and finally in the newly created Department of National Heritage (where there is still little overall strategic cultural policy). And even professionally, it can be argued, the interests of the public library service are certainly not the key priority of the Library Association, in which public librarians are in a minority.

The public library network, therefore, has had no equivalent body to the Arts Council, the Sports Council, or the Museums and Galleries Commission to argue centrally for its support and development, even though it is a locally delivered service. The fact is that these national policy bodies have been successful in promoting their respective causes. The Arts Council did successfully promote the case for the role of the arts in economic regeneration through its support for the Policy Studies Institute report *The economic importance of the arts*, for example.[1] It has kept arts funding and arts issues (including the more "difficult" but important issues of disability arts, ethnic minority arts) in the public eye and in the pages of the national press. Similarly, the Sports Council with its "Sport for All" campaign, its research and advocacy documents, has successfully changed the image of sport from being almost exclusively the concern of professional male athletes and footballers to one of popular jogging, over-50s' swimming and general fitness campaigns. Museums in the 1980s changed their image completely, from being dusty archives to tourist destinations, heritage and interpretation centres, through assiduous promotion, absorbing new skills into the profession and becoming much more entrepreneurial.

Public libraries need this kind of advocacy and promotion very badly. At present it can be argued that their current weak public image is compounded by campaigns such as National Library Week that tend to emphasize cuts in services, a rather bland set of endorsements by

47

middle-of-the-road celebrities and entertainers, and that come across more like "This Week's Charity" than a powerful argument for what is potentially the most important cultural and educational network that will take us into the twenty-first century. The public library's finest moments in recent years – in terms of public relations – have been in response to a number of civil disasters such as the Hungerford shootings in 1987 and the North Wales floods of 1990. The community librarian at Hungerford at the time of the shootings there, Susan Broughton, quickly collected together material from other civil disasters such as the Bradford fire and the *Herald of Free Enterprise* sinking, on issues of bereavement counselling, lists of relevant organizations such as CRUSE and the Tragedy Fund, and the library became a "crisis centre" for that community immediately after the tragedy. She won several awards for her work at Hungerford and has since advised and provided materials to other libraries in response to subsequent civil disasters such as the Kings Cross fire, the Maidenhead school tragedy and others. The actual role of the public library network as Britain's "fourth emergency service", to steal the phrase, is a powerful reminder of what libraries can and often do achieve.[2]

PART 3

The "libraryness" of libraries

CHAPTER 7

What makes libraries special?

Quite apart from its "public" nature, one of the main difficulties of this study has been to define what a library is and what its purpose should be. This might sound strange, because there is a common understanding that libraries are about lending books. Most people know what a library is and know that to enter and inhabit that space involves a number of unspoken rules and assumptions. What is this "libraryness" factor, where does it come from, and what effect does the "libraryness" of libraries have on the way we think about their future?

"Libraryness" partly derives from the large-scale presence of books, which themselves historically evince a quasi-religious or spiritual aura. The first libraries were based in monasteries, as "part of the fabric of the church", according to Thomas Kelly; books and libraries imply a contemplative life; the burning of books is regarded as an affront to human values.[1] Libraries are in some senses seen as quasi-sacred places. But there are other general attributes accepted as part of the library:

- The rule of silence, though no longer insisted upon, remains an unwritten and shared understanding; few other institutions share this rule. This reinforces the idea of the quiet haven in a sea of urban noise.
- The library is seen as being informed with the historical principle of "the right to know", of civic rights, of the freedom of knowledge; it embodies the idea of human betterment, as was described in the earlier chapter on enlightenment.
- The library is regarded as democratic, non-partisan, above sectional interests, inhabiting the "value-free" world of scholarship and general interest.

– Its espousal and encouragement of early childhood literacy and enjoyment of reading are seen as a welcoming entry for the young into civil society and "the great book of life"; the library's role in creating and sustaining literacy cannot be overestimated.

– The library is still seen as a "window on the world", where newspapers can be read, the events of the day absorbed and followed, and where the latest reference books and novels keep the local community in touch with the wider world.

– Librarians enjoy a reputation for being non-judgemental, unlike their peers in other cultural institutions who may adopt partisan artistic positions as a matter of professional and artistic principle.

– Libraries are regarded as highly "porous" institutions in that there are no hard and fixed boundaries to what kinds of materials or information they may stock: books, CDs, videos, leaflets, toys, paintings, newspapers, on-line employment information, etc.

– The library space is regarded as a sanctuary, a place where one may sit, read, browse, sleep and remain unharassed; nobody is judged and therefore nobody is found wanting. It is often one of the few places in a busy city centre where people, particularly women, of all ages go alone and spend time without worry.

– On the other hand, the self-effacing culture of librarians can lead to assumptions of *laissez-faire* and institutional dullness; that librarians are simply anonymous service staff, without opinions or values of their own.

This quality of "libraryness" is historically rich and widely understood. It is one of the great institutional strengths of the public library service, and has proved resilient and self-renewing. Yet the weight of this history may hinder the capacity of librarians to develop a fresh perspective on where libraries could be going in the future.

Library buildings are social objects

The first public libraries may now seem to have been austere and forbidding places. Their dark interiors and hidden stacks of books implied that the storage and classification of books was their primary function, but they were also symbols of the beginnings and ideals of public access to knowledge and education. The history of public libraries (and their future) embodies crucial themes of social democracy; of ideas about universal suffrage; government by informed consent; equality of opportunity and the rights of the individual. Modern buildings and bright interiors continue to reflect ideals of intellectual rights, the centrality of education in our society and the role of public libraries in helping to sustain a public realm. But the last 150 years have also seen dramatic changes in the relations between production, distribution and consumption of culture. We are still in the very early stages of even more profound changes envisaged by the proliferation of electronic forms of communication. These changes will inevitably affect public libraries and our ideas about the public realm.

The transformation in book production, and the move towards electronic forms, is likely to bring with it changes in the way our current categories of knowledge are organized and classified. The changing world of the production and distribution of knowledge presents fundamental long-term challenges to public libraries as places that organize and present knowledge and information. In turn, public library buildings themselves express much about the changing use, function and status of public libraries as places that represent wider collective values.

The premiss of Thomas A. Markus's work on the origin of modern building types in his book *Buildings and power* is that buildings are objects that are primarily socially defined, they are not just abstract designs or simply bricks and mortar: "Everything about a building has social meaning – its form, function and spatial structure are each capable of analysis."[2]

As public places, library buildings in some ways represent values of the public realm – the world of social exchange. They are places that manifest the idea of state support (local and national) for the collective right of access individuals have to knowledge and information.

Municipal power

The municipal public libraries grew from a confident civic culture. They were part of a repertoire of civic buildings and landscapes that reshaped many towns and cities. The town hall, civic halls, the public libraries and museums, the public parks and squares all helped to provide a distinctive character to Victorian British cities. The public libraries of Manchester,

Leeds, Sheffield and Middlesbrough, for example, are grand civic buildings that were part of a strong nineteenth-century municipal self-image. The development of public libraries along with other public facilities – museums, galleries, parks and baths – reflected the economic and political muscle of the new industrial cities, and the emergence of a new municipal government. The tax-paying citizen, the civic city centres, and the new public services and facilities provided formed the centre-piece of the Victorian ideology upon which the social management of industrial cities was based. As Mark Girouard noted in his outstanding study *The English town*:

> If this book has heroes, they are the corporations of Victorian towns, especially northern industrial towns . . . With unfailing energy and resourcefulness they took over services from inefficient private enterprise, and made them prosperous and fruitful, leaving behind them a rich harvest of town halls, court-houses, market halls, schools, viaducts, bridges, reservoirs, and pumping stations, all proudly flaunting the corporation coat-of-arms from ripely ebullient architecture.[3]

The public library was often a centre-piece of this confident era of municipal power.

Philanthropy and self-help

The public library took its shape from a mixture of municipal power, a belief in education as part of a project of social engineering, a recognition of people as citizens, and the emerging idea of public institutions serving a general good. Public libraries represented many of the emerging themes that developed into the foundations of post-war social democracy. They were forward-looking institutions that were part of the move towards social reform, and part of a humanist tradition that saw ignorance as the greatest hindrance to social progress. Public libraries were also adaptable to many Victorian causes and to local attempts to ameliorate what were seen as the excesses of urban proletarian life. They were, for example, part of the temperance movement. Newspapers were provided in libraries as a deliberate attempt to compete with pubs, and, as Thomas Markus notes, easy access was considered vital. In some cases, "everything was done to make the step from the street into the reading room feel like the step into the pub".[4] Public libraries were meant to offer an alternative view of public life in comparison with pubs and other emerging forms of social entertainment available in the developing industrial cities.

Public libraries, however, were fought for at least as much as they were imposed. They grew from the already popular subscription libraries, literary groups, mechanics institutes, miners' welfare associations, workers' education societies and other societies with briefs to promote "useful knowledge". Self-improvement and popular instruction were widespread in the cities of the late 1800s.

The rule of reason

Public libraries were also part of a liberal humanist tradition. Their emergence can be interpreted as the outcome, crudely summarized, of a clash between an emerging philosophy of reason with an older established order based on a closed social hierarchy and ruled by a revealed religious authority. The philosophy of reason stems from the period of Enlightenment and is based on an idea of an open society of individuals where social order rests on a sense of autonomy and rational knowledge. Public libraries sit well with the idea of provision for citizens of a rational social order. The belief in a "reasoning public" feeds into the idea of a public sphere based upon rationality. Jürgen Habermas defines this as the realm of social life in which public opinion, as an expression of the general interest of citizens, is formed. His analysis of democratic theory turns on his understanding of a bourgeois public sphere developing in the eighteenth century in which public debate arose in places that were neither totally private nor directly part of ruling institutions.

Books, printing and a confident literary tradition

Public libraries took hold at a time when print and publishing were in the ascendancy. Thomas Markus suggests that: "The growth of public libraries in the three centuries from the invention of printing was both a cause and a consequence of [the] changed reading habits."[5]

The introduction of printing allowed printed material to have a life away from the place where it was produced (or reproduced). Printed books had a new mobility in time and space. The introduction of printing drove the social shift from orality to literacy. Raymond Williams describes the transition of writing from a function of recording an oral tradition to the stage when nearly all composition was written to be silently read and was generalized as "literature".[6]

Printing also boosted a culture of learning and helped to create new disciplines. However, the introduction of printing brought with it new kinds of licensing and other means of controlling ownership and readership, particularly of the press. In her book *Cultural rights*, Celia Lury traces the emergence and acceptance of the notion of public rights of access to ideas and information and the way this was bound to a constantly evolving division between market and state.

> While the acceptance of this right of access was integral to the emergence of the ideal of the public sphere as the site of communication, reflection and decision making, in actuality this right was defined restrictively in relation to the rights of the individual either as citizen of the bourgeois *polis* or consumer in cultural markets.[7]

She argues that the proliferation of printing and its regulation are one of the initial moments of an internal division in cultural reproduction between the interests of the state and the market. In other words, the development in printing was neither completely determined by a free market nor totally regulated by the state, but each position appealed to people in different ways. It was a division that created opposing conceptions of an audience as either a public or a market. The division between citizen and consumer clearly still has powerful resonances today.

Books were to form the basis of a legitimate, shared national literary culture. The public library in Newham in London, for example, has the names of Milton, Shakespeare and other revered authors picked out in bas-relief on the brickwork of the building. The Linenhall Library in Belfast (a subscription library) has stained-glass windows depicting Burke, Swift and other literary figures. Many other nineteenth-century public buildings are decorated with literary icons. The certainty with which these figures were incorporated into the physical fabric of the building reflects a confidence in this literary tradition and the wish to promote it. The difference between the terms "literate" and "literacy" suggests that literacy means more than an ability to read, it implies the reading of those books included within the literary tradition. In fact, it could be argued that public libraries helped to shape a particular literary culture that excluded the burgeoning mass of cheap novels and pamphlets that were available in the pubs, coffee houses, tobacconists and commercial reading rooms of the mid- to late 1800s. Public libraries encouraged a distinctive approach to learning, knowledge and literature, *one that appealed to an idea of citizenship above that of the consumer.*

In this way, libraries began to represent the idea that there was a shared, common, even a public set of disciplines of knowledges, and were a repository for a public social memory based upon print and books rather than oral traditions. Futurologists such as Alvin Toffler see public libraries as part of a transformative period when social memories began to be stored outside the human brain. In his book *The third wave* he argues that:

> Second Wave civilisation smashed the memory barrier. It spread mass literacy. It kept systematic business records. It built thousands of libraries and museums. It invented the file cabinet. In short it moved social memory outside the skull, found new ways to store it, and thus expanded it beyond previous limits.[8]

Classification

The expansion of empires, theories of evolution and the growth of science and medicine rested in part on ambitious programmes of classification. Classification of the world was a major preoccupation of the Victorian era that saw the detailed and vigorous exploration of the world, of science and of the human body. This preoccupation is reflected in the design and organization of many Victorian institutions such as schools, hospitals, museums, zoos, public libraries and public parks, where people, illnesses, artefacts, animals, books and plants were defined, arranged and exhibited. The early botanical gardens, many of which are still a focus of civic attraction today – in Belfast, Sheffield and in many other cities – displayed exotic flora from around the world.

Classification is, of course, more than the arrangement of texts in a library, it is an expression of a system of thought or philosophy. The Victorian emphasis on classification was linked to a notion of evolution and the idea of the linearity and direct progression of historical evolutionary time. The Victorian forms of knowledge reveal a voyage of self-discovery, a reassessment of the inner world or a search for self-knowledge. McGrane argues in his study of the emergence of anthropology that classification of the world and other (non-European) civilizations and populations was above all a quest for self-knowledge.[9] Classification also tended to be a particularly Protestant affair, as was the autodidactic culture and that of silent reading.

The design of public libraries

The early public libraries embodied these themes of enlightenment, learning, knowledge and classification, and these themes were reflected in the design and architecture of the buildings. As well as the direct architectural and ornamental references to key literary and historical figures, library buildings symbolized the aspirations that the library and its contents of knowledge hoped to satisfy. So, for example, the journey from a state of darkness and ignorance to light and enlightenment is consciously represented in the design of Stockholm's central library (although it was not built until the 1920s). From the street entrance, visitors can glimpse the sky-lit dome through the dark passage and stairways. The light-filled dome represents a state of rational transcendence reached by learning. The metaphor of a personal journey from a state of ignorance to one of wisdom is also illustrative of a particular view of human progress where history is seen as a story of continuous improvement.

The library dome is also a feature of the Central Library in Manchester and, very famously, the Reading Room of the British Library. The dome seems to represent the physical space for the individual's silent reading and thought, and could be said to mimic the shape of the empty skull. The dome is, as Markus points out, also a metaphor for universal knowledge and can be traced back to Rome's Pantheon, representing divine order.

The public library was almost like a secular cathedral, emerging at a time when citizens began to be recognized as having individual rights and consciousnesses. Books, unlike oral traditions, were directed at individuals. The icons and symbols of medieval religions were partially replaced by the printed Bible. The great frescoes to be found in the churches of Renaissance Italy were put there to tell stories from the Bible in a visual language for those who could not read. In his article on the new Bibliothèque de France, Anthony Vidler reflects upon Victor Hugo's assertion in 1831 in *Notre Dame de Paris* that: "This will kill that. The book will kill the building. That is to say printing will kill architecture."[10]

Vidler suggests that Hugo's argument is more or less correct, and that the symbolic power of the cathedral, the priest and the prince to teach by means of sign and symbol was partially undermined by the mobile propaganda of books. The visual pictorial stories and icons demonstrating social hierarchies and religious laws were part and parcel of religious, and other, buildings. The primacy of these visual codes began to be undermined by print and reading and the notion of individual consciousness. Architecture had begun to lose its primary role as a kind of "social book". "From the time of Gutenberg, architecture had suffered a progressive loss of cultural power and significant form in proportion to the implacable ascendance of the book, which second 'Tower of Babel' had found its popular audience and political role in the nineteenth century."[11]

Books and the rise of print-based culture may have signalled the clash between image-based and word-based religious involvement. While the symbolic power of architecture may have changed, libraries still represent, as Markus suggests, an archetypal building form for providing knowledge that was dominant through the nineteenth and much of the twentieth century. The public library is both a place for ideas and an idea itself, it organizes public access to books. Money and status were invested in libraries.

> Since knowledge is power one should not be surprised by the huge investment in these buildings and their contents by the state, city authorities, Royalty and aristocracy, learned societies, and churches . . . And once the working class organised to obtain power, it, too, invested capital in knowledge.[12]

The public library, therefore, embodies a principle of rights of access to knowledge and the power that the acquisition of knowledge implies.

CHAPTER 8

The era of light and glass

In the 150 years or so since they were first established, public libraries have been moulded and adapted to meet the needs of a changing world. But they have not yet been superseded. As archetypal buildings or prototypes, public libraries still have a powerful resonance.

Contemporary libraries are founded upon a range of old and new ideas about what libraries are and how they function. Old ideas took on new meanings. The idea of encouraging the rational citizen to acquire knowledge and learning was refracted through the lens of social democracy to become universal provision for an educated democracy. Universal provision has been a powerful idea that has been given symbolic form in contemporary library design.

For many librarians we talked to, the ideal library should be as open as possible, and the interiors clearly visible from the outside. Glass and transparency reveal the universal and democratic ideals bound up in the idea of a public library. The desire for openness also reflects a wish to reduce any barriers to entry. The threshold has to be low, the sightlines clear and the public areas deep. The point of high visibility is to reveal the presence of people inside the library as much as it is to show books. The library is a social place as much as a storehouse for books. In contrast to earlier public libraries or reading rooms, most of the books are now directly accessible from the shelves. The books available on the shelves outnumber those in closed stockrooms in the back. The public areas of the library now include most of the building. The private areas – the staff rooms, stockrooms and book repair rooms – are kept invisible. The library has to make a statement that it is a public building and not simply a building to which there is limited public access. Therefore, modern library buildings appear accessible and open; the secret, authoritarian, professional areas are kept to a minimum. These ideals are clear in many modern public libraries such as those we visited in Bromley, Croydon, Enfield, Hartlepool, Hounslow, Islington (Mildmay Library), Lewisham ("Wavelengths"), Omagh, Woking and others.

The public desk or reception area is now a standard feature of most public buildings and office buildings. The reception desk sets the tone and atmosphere of the foyer and the building. The role of staff behind the desk is both to provide guidance and monitor people entering the building. Many office buildings prioritize the security factors, using uniformed staff and clearly signalling the intention to keep uninvited people out and to protect those within. Libraries, also, have installed anti-theft electronic turnstiles. The reception desk serves to provide a vantage point from which staff can monitor users and exert a subtle influence over public behaviour. The library desk also has to reflect a sense of public access and openness. Many libraries identify these areas as "customer services", and have introduced to the library customer service staff (often in discreet uniform) who fulfil a reception function. This role is one of managing public use of the building and has an influence on the sense of public space the building creates. Some modern libraries achieve a similar sense of interior space as that created by airports, new stations, banks, shopping centres and modern office blocks. Places where the smiling stewardess, the bank clerk or the receptionist presents a new face for a "public" space where customer service is everything.

Gulten Wagner in her semiotic study of Australian public libraries presents a detailed analysis of the interior spatial arrangement of the library. She argues that the foyer area is a powerful control point and that electronic surveillance devices for a library's materials are usually installed in this area. However, for her, it is the circulation desk that is "an unmistakable signifier of this institution". She goes on to argue that: "The prominence of the Circulation Desk over the Information Desk, as the site of material exchange activity between users and the library system, signifies the prominence of Recreation over Information."[1]

For many regular library users, the returns trolley – the place where books just returned by readers are temporarily placed – is the first place to browse. The only thing that these books have in common is that they have just been read. The returns trolley is the part of the library where users get a direct sense of what others are reading. The books just brought back have an immediate recommendation attached that distinguishes them from other books anonymously arranged on the shelves. The fascination for the returns trolley is more than the eccentric behaviour of library users, it demonstrates the latent interest in what others are reading and the scope for libraries to develop innovative ways to present books and build upon reader interests. The returns trolley also demonstrates a sense of openness in the working of the library. The process of bringing books back and reshelving can take place in the public areas and users can intervene and extract books before they are replaced on the shelves.

Despite the contemporary use of glass, the transparency and the brightly coloured fixtures and furnishing, the rules of social behaviour in the library are still informed with the requirement that stood for decades, namely that people should be (predominantly) silent in the library. The request for "silence please", along with the banishment of drinking, smoking, gambling and the racing pages of the newspapers, was part of the ambience constructed to make the library distinct from other public social or commercial places. Few libraries now demand total silence from their users and the ambience created by interior design and management has changed. Nevertheless, in many public libraries a "cloistered" atmosphere still prevails, and is clearly valued amidst the noise and frenetic pace of urban life without.

Every public library is different

Despite these general themes of openness and rights to information and universal provision, there are many forms of public libraries, each saying something different.

There is the modern civic library incorporated into the post-war town hall buildings. In a public library such as that in Merton where the library and the town hall are one and the same building, the qualities of the library are linked to local government and citizenship. The library is physically linked to local government, local democracy and a sense of civic leadership.

The planning of the new towns usually included a public library: in fact Redcliffe Maud in his work on the form of local government and new towns suggested that each new town should have a public library. Along with the new schools and health services, it was a facility that helped to define the new towns' distinct civic identities. The new library in Crawley was built as part of a complex called County Buildings that opened in 1963. It also housed a police station and a medical clinic, and was planned to be opposite the technical college. The complex was designed by the County Council planners and was based around a little central civic courtyard and civic fountain (which, however, quickly became a car-park).

There are dozens of small community libraries that resemble domestic interiors rather than anything "institutional" associated with the local or national state. In some of these, the library is used throughout as a public building, with users and community groups able to use staff work rooms or book repair rooms for meetings, play groups and dozens of other activities. In some instances, library users are able to make themselves a cup of tea before settling down to read, and community groups may even borrow a key so that they can use the building late into the evening. The library in Thorntree in Middlesbrough, Cleveland, for example, which was one of those studied, is decorated with potted plants and children's toys brought in by the staff. Every attempt has been made to give the library a bright, attractive, homely feel.

There are many instances of libraries built into redbrick leisure centre complexes during the 1970s. The library may be next door to a roller rink, as is the library in Welwyn Garden City; or it may be under the same roof as a swimming pool, as in the case of the library in Lewisham's "Wavelengths" in Deptford. The public library in these instances is associated with purpose-built leisure facilities.

During the 1980s, libraries were built into new covered shopping centres and took on some of the design features of the shopping centre. Hounslow Library is part of the Treaty Shopping Centre and forms one side of the main indoor square. The glass walls present bold window displays, and the library interior (particularly the children's library) is clearly visible. Inside, the lighting, the open-plan layout, the colour scheme, the subtle staff dress code, the escalator and tannoy announcements, and even the signposting and presentation of the book, video and CD stock resemble the look and feel of a department store. On a smaller scale, there is the example of a local library in Norton, a village in Cleveland, close to Stockton, which occupies a converted supermarket. Some of the design features of the supermarket have been adapted to

63

library use. The sign formats and lighting arrangements of the former supermarket now suit a modern local library.

What does the public library in the form of a department store or supermarket say about the changing nature of the public realm and the way in which people relate to public services? One answer to this question is to say that public expression has been subsumed within a now dominant consumer culture. Another might be to say that the attempt to make the library as welcoming as possible has demonstrated that public buildings can reassert a dominant identity in an otherwise commercial environment. The library in the Treaty Centre in Hounslow not only adds a distinct and different dimension to the shopping centre, but in fact also makes a contribution to the commercial success of the centre, as neighbouring retailers have agreed.

The prevalence of domestic style interiors, especially within smaller public libraries, points to the predominance of women amongst library staff and the way in which female staff have helped to create a sense of hospitality, or, as Gulten Wagner describes, women in public librarianship support the library's role as a nurturing institution of the state. The prevalence of women amongst library staff and the effect this has on public perceptions of the service has barely been addressed by the library profession, in which most senior positions are held by men. Gulten Wagner argues that the gendered nature of the institution is part of the reason why the library service has been ignored. She goes on to suggest that the traditional role of the library as a nurturing institution comes into conflict with its role as a signifier of the information age, a role that has a more masculine image.

Citizens or customers?

Public libraries, like many other public institutions – town halls, hospitals, colleges, museums – adopted a consumer language. The Citizen's Charter redefines the relationship between citizens and public services as a contractual or commercial transaction. Habermas's definition of the public realm refers to citizens considering matters of general interest. The shift of accountability from citizen to customer removes the level of general interest and focuses accountability towards the customer's

private economic concerns. As with these other institutions, the requirement of a universal service to prove universal use has been overlaid with
current management philosophies to make certain that services are "customer driven". The approach of the public library to individual citizens
has changed. The individual self-improving citizen of Victorian public
libraries has been reshaped more in the mould of a customer. The citizen
is revalued as a taxpayer and therefore a customer of services.

Public libraries have been a centre-piece of local government and
frequently the most popular local service. The decline in local government has inevitably affected the identity of the library service. The
changing relationship between public and private, and between citizens
and consumers, has been played out through libraries themselves. The
smaller libraries that are made to look like domestic interiors appeal to
the other private identity of individuals: the privacy of being at home.
The civic version of the public realm is losing ground both to the private
consumer and to the private home. Private homes are increasingly
part of the market for more and new cultural and communication technologies.

Studies of the use of television in the home show that viewers often
begin discussions of public issues sparked off by TV programmes; these
are then continued through their wider social networks. Thus, it can be
argued that the nature of the public sphere as the realm in which matters
of general interest are discussed is changing rather than disappearing.
While some commentators argue that electronic communication undermines the idea of public life, others argue that new kinds of public interaction engendered by electronic networks can create new kinds of
electronic public space.[2]

The irony of the library designed as a department store and emulating
the visual design of the shopping world is that the library member can
walk out with a £100 worth of books, CDs and videos – for a minimal
fee. The library service still holds to a welfare state model based upon
collective general provision. Yet questions of charging for services, and
of tailoring the service to particular target groups within the population,
have begun to challenge the idea of blanket universal provision. Public
libraries walk a fine line between a commercial and a public world, and
the competing languages of citizenship and consumption, which often
produces stresses and strains in library management philosophies and
policies.

Storehouse to social centre

The increased attention given to people as consumers has been reflected in public libraries. In particular, libraries located within shopping centres, and which share some of the shops' design values, often carry this over to the presentation of the books. The book stock may be presented along the same lines as merchandise to be bought – under the themed headings of thrillers, sagas, romances. Reorganizing the library stock along these lines emphasizes the growing prominence of a consumer language and the difficulties with the traditional approach to classifying the library stock. The Dewey decimal system was designed as a tool for librarians – people with the skills to define and classify knowledge and information – at a time when library book stacks were not generally open to the public. The problem is not simply that knowledge and media formats have expanded beyond the point at which the Dewey system can cope. It is both a philosophical issue to do with reclassifying knowledge, and a question of how physically to arrange the books and other media in a way that makes the library more than an unintelligible book warehouse. In the organization and presentation of books, libraries help to make sense of the knowledge they hold.

The problem of where to put books in a library that promotes and displays its stock is constant. The very physical presence of books in a fixed space presents a problem – how do you arrange them – as Thomas Markus points out, despite the use of hypertexts or multidimensional data bases, "as long as the books are on the shelf the issue remains".[3] For public libraries it is more than a classification problem, it is also about how to present and interpret a library stock for public use. If a public library looks like Blockbuster Videos it may appear to discredit its status as a public service (many would question the validity of public subsidy for such a service), and the distinction between a free and paid-for cultural service is difficult to sustain. If, on the other hand, a public library appears as a dusty, archaic, forbidding institution, then it can be argued that it lacks popular appeal and cannot claim to be providing a widely used universal service. Similarly, if a library presents its stock in the same consumer terms as, for example, a Virgin Megastore, then it can be accused of following a consumer culture in which the audience is divided up according to taste: people are country and western fans or lovers of horror, and literature is designated as "the classics". And yet professional and academic classification systems are difficult to translate into coherent physical arrangements of books on shelves in ways that are accessible to library users. Again the library, which is a mixed market institution, is inevitably caught in the constant flux between public and private.

Books and information

If the rise of printing and the appearance of the mass-produced "book" threatened the cultural power of architecture, as Victor Hugo predicted, then the rise of electronic means of distribution threatens both the cultural power of the book and the building that contains it. The rise and dominance of print and publishing is reflected in a strong literary tradition, and public libraries were part of the formation and regulation of this tradition and the widespread belief in the value of a literary culture. The "book" form has been more than a method of distribution of information – it has underpinned the whole liberal conception of cultural authority. Many commentators now suggest that this print-based culture is under threat. New forms of electronic distribution threaten the previously settled relationship between author and reader mediated by the book. Howard Bloch and Carla Hesse, in their introduction to a special edition of the American journal *Representations* on the French Bibliothèque, state that:

> The potential loss of the book, the disappearance of the author and reader as coherent imagined selves constituted through the stabilising form of the bound book, the disordering of authorial agency in favour of an increasingly active reader (or alternatively, the empowerment of the "on-line" author in control of the uses and distribution of texts), . . . the transformation of copyright into contract: all point toward the subsuming fear of a loss of community.[4]

A classification meltdown – a breakdown of existing forms, genres and the boundaries between different classes of knowledge (for example, between science and art) – is threatened, or promised, to arrive with new forms of electronic or microelectronic means of reproduction and distribution. For some, there are new possibilities of going beyond traditional divisions between science and arts, suggesting the potential of more encyclopaedic forms of knowledge. A common feature of all these kinds of scenarios is a new meaning attributed to the term "information". For example, information has developed a new significance as a resource for capital accumulation. The old equation of knowledge and power is overlaid by a newer equation between information and money. Although the term "information" is very widely and generally used (and is perhaps the most appropriate word available), it seems inadequate to describe the scope of change said to be happening in the development, circulation and application of new knowledges.

The imperfect classificatory terms "fiction" and "non-fiction" began to be replaced in library circles by the term "information" twenty or more years ago. The phrase "books and information" was a useful way of generally describing the services of the library and it acknowledges that much of what is housed in libraries is not in book form. The term also highlights an "informing" role for the library providing material on general matters from EEC legislation to lists of local doctors' surgeries. In this context, it is the use-value that matters. For this reason, information as a category of knowledge does not generally attract cultural value judgements. It is this neutral quality of the term that was convenient for the library profession wishing to move away from the value judgements bound up in earlier literary and educational traditions.

However, "information" has also become a blanket term to describe everything; it is used to refer to bus timetables, language tapes and the novels of Virginia Woolf. As a descriptive word it provides a way of equalizing the contents of a library. Everything is information in some form or other, it has a potential use-value for someone. The term also confirms the role of the librarian as an information scientist, a person who knows how to find, extract and store information but does not appear to make any judgements about the (cultural) value of the "information" itself.

The instrumental "informative" sense of the term "information" helps to conflate form and content. Information can be directions given in the street or the most up-to-date share prices. What is important is its instrumental use-value. The priority given to use-value implies that information is free-floating stuff that finds a format to exist within. Whether it is in book form, CD or video is of little consequence. Each is a neutral format holding "information". This sense of detachment of form from content contrasts with the (still common) valorization of the book as an object.

There is now a consensus that developments in communication technology and the new links between information technology and wealth creation will have far-reaching effects and will inevitably change the operating environment of the public library service. For futurologists such as Alvin Toffler, the public library is an institution of the "second wave" industrial civilization, as noted earlier. However, he argues that the second wave is not yet an entirely spent force since it overlaps with the emergence of the "third wave", a new civilization that has been called "the information age", or "the post industrial age". The all-encompassing term "information" is a stopgap term, a bridge from here to there. Public libraries have been and still are part of this information world. However, the excitement around ideas of tele-cottages or millennium projects conjuring up imaginary communication centres are largely bypassing existing public library debates.

And so . . .

Electronic communication is generally seen to accelerate a shift of the public realm from physical places to an existence in the airwaves and reception in private domestic homes. And yet there is a concurrent fear of the loss of community and the loss of a realm where general opinion can be formed. There is still a desire for informal social space. The Swedish approach to the design of libraries – to represent public living-rooms or open squares – is simply a contemporary expression of the long-standing wish to regard libraries as built versions of the public realm. The County Library in Skaraborg, Sweden, is designed as a covered public square. The square has street lamps, and signposting and a symbolic tree of knowledge at its centre. It also provides space for cultural activities and performances. The attempt to create new kinds of public space is also apparent in some new office designs such as the new Manchester headquarters of the British Council that emphasize public areas rather than private workspace. In fact, the office world is rediscovering a version of public space and trying to incorporate a communal feel into progressive office design. These buildings reflect a new value attached to social interaction, and a recognition that "work" gets done away from desks, in the places where chance encounters with colleagues and social exchanges can and do take place.

The underlying principle of the public library as creating an accessible realm of knowledge remains at the heart of the reorganization of information and the public realm. But the public library service remains trapped in old forms of organization – the buildings, professional hierarchy and its current relationship with local government. In order to be the service stations on the information highway of the future, public libraries need to re-establish their basis as a resource for individuals. This is likely to mean finding a role in supporting future learning and education programmes. They also need to re-establish a social role. Public libraries might offer facilities to support community groups, self-help and voluntary groups and provide a resource for the kind of social activity and sense of community in ways that enhance the "age of information". Public libraries remain archetypal buildings, places that recognize the rights and interests of the private individual in a public world.

PART 4

Spheres of influence

It seems to us that the public library service in Britain today operates in five main areas of public policy, or spheres of influence. We describe these as:

1. Libraries and urban vitality
2. The invisible web: the public library and social policy
3. Education and life-long learning
4. Information and the right to know
5. Other worlds: libraries, fiction and popular reading

CHAPTER 9

Libraries and urban vitality

The research itself grew out of an earlier Comedia study on urban vitality, the *Out of Hours* study of 1991, which looked into the social, economic and cultural life of 12 towns in Britain. That study concentrated on town centres as focal points of local civic culture, as transport hubs, as retailing, commercial and civic centres, as magnets for night-life and entertainment, and as the places in which most unique local identities had been forged, architecturally and historically. That study attempted to chart the "social vitality" of urban centres in contemporary Britain, and to outline the problems that prevented them from becoming safe, accessible and welcoming to all sections of the community. Once again, in brief, it was about the quality of the local public realm.

It was precisely this study that alerted us to the central importance of public libraries as perhaps the most continuously successful focal points of democratic local life. This role, we came to realize, was one that had been underplayed by librarians themselves. Yet the library is for many people a primary reason for coming into the town centre, and for spending some time – for free – checking out the latest journals, magazines and newspapers, picking up leaflets about events and activities, browsing through the returns trolley, and (in some libraries) having a coffee and meeting friends. If our emphasis on the quality of this informal "browsing" culture as one of the key attributes to successful towns and cities seems overly "European" – a criticism often levelled against advocates of this kind of urbanity – then again it is worth recalling Girouard reminding the British that the social promenade was invented in Britain, and the landscaping of urban walks admired throughout Europe:

The English have lost the habit of social walking, once as common in Britain as the *passeggiatas* of Continental Europe. But in the eighteenth century malls, parades, walks, promenades or esplanades were the outdoor counterpart of assembly rooms, the places where polite society came "to see or be seen".

Browsing

Glancing through books, grazing along the shelves and displays is an activity thoroughly associated with libraries and bookshops. Since the introduction of open shelves rather than closed stacks, browsing has become one of the main things people do in libraries. Studies such as the one carried out by Deborah Goodall for her report *Browsing in public libraries* showed that the process of browsing plays a major part in a reader's selection of books.[1]

The case-study work showed that browsing as an activity contributed to the feel and atmosphere of libraries. Library users described the library as relaxing and peaceful. They also described the sensation of losing track of time when browsing and for some it created almost a dreamlike state. Browsing is an unpressured, non-instrumental activity that can be creative, leading to new discoveries and the making of new connections, but it is also a useful way of making sense of the library and finding out about its stock. Browsing is rarely a completely random activity. The research suggested that library users were keen quickly to find the sections they were interested in and then spend a bit of time browsing. Library users suggested that it was by browsing that they kept up to date with a subject or explored an author. As Deborah Goodall concludes in her research, the fact that so many people use the library by browsing makes the presentation and arrangement of books a critical issue for library professionals. But it has wider implications.

Urban vitality

The qualities of browsing in a library or bookshops – unhurried perusal, unexpected discoveries, an openness to new possibilities, exploring interests – are also characteristic of being in an urban setting where people window-shop, stroll and keep in touch with what's going on. These qualities and ways of being in and using urban landscapes are now being recognized by planners and town centre managers in their attempts to make city centres more attractive and usable. For example, the ease of walking, the dimensions of a town centre, a mix of attractions and features, the sense of safety, all help to determine a sense of urban vitality.

The questions of urban vitality and how to create safer city centres and reverse the monoculture imposed by the closed-in shopping malls were considered in many urban regeneration strategies. The attempt to recover vitality centred on rediscovering the town centre for people. The new squares, festivals, canalside walks and town centre housing policies were all intended to encourage people into town and to feel safe in numbers. The city centre was to be a stage upon which urban life was played and the non-instrumental activities – sitting, waiting, chatting, reading and watching – were all part of the milieu.

There are similarities between browsing in the library and browsing in streets, squares and shops. And yet, the contribution of public libraries to the vitality of town or city centres has not been recognized. City centre libraries attract people. They generate a flow of people through the library doors from the moment they open until they close and yet public libraries were not seen as part of the attempt to increase the activity and vitality of town centres in the 1980s.

The failure to understand the potential public libraries could offer city centres represents a major missed opportunity both for urban regeneration and for the library world. Public libraries are one of the most popular cultural institutions with much to offer town centres. They attract people and add to the diversity of the centre, they are relatively safe places and often stay open into the evening (but perhaps not late enough!). Libraries also promote and support other venues, their programmes and city centre events. Their inclusion within city centre regeneration may have lessened the arguments now levelled against some city centre strategies that seem to have favoured business elites and minority cultural interests over the needs of the residential population. The library world also lost an opportunity to make new connections, to think again about the role and relevance of public libraries and to reassert and re-establish the library at the heart of the town centre.

The Birmingham factor

The main focus of the Birmingham case study was the "invisibility" of the library to planners and those concerned with the economic status of the city centre as a whole. The Central Library lies at the heart of its city centre strategy area, but it is never mentioned in the publicity about the success of that urban regeneration initiative. For example, the Council's "City Centre Strategy" of 1992 mentions the city's "theatres, its museums and art gallery, the City of Birmingham Symphony Orchestra and new festivals . . . the Royal Ballet and the D'Oyly Carte Opera Company" as all having contributed to the life of the city. But no mention of the Central Library. Similarly, handsome new signposting in and around Centenary Square, Victoria Square and Chamberlain Square points visitors and residents to many different features and attractions – except the Central Library. If one stands in the magnificently refurbished Centenary Square looking east, the whole of the east "wall" of the square is taken up by a large civic building, with not a single piece of signposting, name plate or decorative panel or banner telling you that this is, indeed, the Central Library, the largest lending library, in fact, in Europe.

A survey of attendance figures at city centre institutions was compiled (see Table 9.1). This confirms that Birmingham Central Library is responsible for the highest amount of daily "people-activity" of all public facilities in the city centre. It should therefore have been regarded as pivotal in any discussions about the further animation of the city centre.

This lack of visibility denies the important role of the public library and its potential in civic and economic renewal. The connection between browsing in the library and browsing out in the city has been made by Sarah Rabkin who teaches at the University of California.

Perhaps the most magical urban spaces of all, at least to me, are bookstores and libraries. If I were an architect or planner I think I would pay close attention to the places where books are bought and borrowed. Buildings that house books unite two kinds of architecture, literal and literary, and I suspect they can teach us a lot about how to create environments full of hope and goodwill . . . . In the best one-of-a-kind book shops, as in the most enticing outdoor landscapes, mystery and possibility are written into every nook and corner.[2]

Table 9.1   Monthly attendance figures.

Birmingham City Museum & Art Gallery (free entrance)	61,000
Birmingham City Museum of Science & Industry (free entrance)	33,000
Birmingham Cathedral (free entrance)	4,200
Birmingham City Central Library (free entrance)	*151,000*
Birmingham Repertory Theatre (paying visitors)	10,700
International Convention Centre (casual and paying visitors)	83,300
National Indoor Arena (paying ticket-holders)	37,500

The presence of public libraries in town centres not only contributes to the general vitality of the town centre by attracting people but, as the Comedia research suggests, by doing so also helps to sustain the shopping areas.

The impact of the library on town centre retailing

Hounslow Central Library was built in 1988 as a cornerstone of the new Treaty Shopping Centre. The library is part of a larger complex – or "*kulturhus*" as the Scandinavians might say – called Centre Space. As well as the library, there is a performance venue, a café and a leisure services shop. The public library is on one level on the second floor. The library is a very busy library. It is used by an average of 2,500 people a day and often around 4,500 people on Saturdays.

Our own observation exercises showed that there were approximately 130 people in the library at any one time. The coffee bar in Centre Space is busy all day long. Centre Space adds much to the health and vitality of the Treaty Shopping Centre, a fact that the other retailers in the centre – initially very sceptical about the library – now unanimously welcome and support as a dynamic feature. Survey evidence showed that over half the people using the library were combining library use with a shopping trip. Our interviews showed that in both Birmingham and Hounslow young people are likely to make visits to the library with friends or to meet friends.

The case study for Dorset County Council required an assessment of possible locations for a new central library in Bournemouth. One possible location was in the main shopping area. Surveys were carried out amongst retailers in Weymouth and Hartlepool – other towns where libraries had been relocated to central shopping areas – to assess the economic impact of these libraries on the surrounding retail trade. The surveys sought to establish whether the business of shops had in any way been affected by the opening of the library. The following conclusions emerged:

- Property developers, estate agents and the investment community were largely unaware of the role that libraries could play in strengthening shopping centres. The view that emerged was that libraries only became significant when they were part of planning gain negotiations. As someone noted *"I only think of libraries when the local authority discusses planning gain."*
- In general, retailers were relatively unaware of the library as an attraction drawing people into a shopping area. However, some commented that but for the library their situation in the recession may have been still worse. The advantage of the library may become more apparent in the recession, although that is more difficult to quantify. Yet we were told at a seminar in South London by one librarian that "when Blackheath Library closes on a Wednesday the shops go dead".

The survey concluded, however, that perhaps now a threshold has been reached. An increasing number of developers who were interviewed in a second round of interviews noted that putting libraries into shopping centres may be a way of revitalizing centres that are either declining or because of the recession have not yet got off the ground. This is supported by evidence from librarians themselves who have noted a more positive attitude, and where, in some instances, deals are being suggested involving peppercorn rents to get libraries to relocate.

There are some positive messages for the library to take away from the survey. Key shops noted significant increases in turnover after the opening of a library near them. However, although shopkeepers have a broadly positive view of the library, they are not aware of the substantial amounts of people who visit them nor of their economic impacts. They note the increased footfall, but do not make the connection between this and increased turnover or stable turnover when there is a general decline. Clearly, the library also benefits when it is part of a shopping centre. Perhaps the time has come for the library world to spell out in more detail to shopkeepers how libraries can enhance the economic and social vitality of the town or city centre. One of the most obvious ways is by highlighting the role that many libraries play in promoting local tourism.

The public library and tourism

Because the public library often houses the local archives – documentary, photographic, personal – and often acts as a small publisher of material of local interest (such as facsimile documents and posters, reproductions of old local photographic postcards and so on), it is also a magnet for local residents and visitors. Similarly, because people go to libraries in the expectation of seeking information there, many libraries also act officially or unofficially as local tourist centres. In some places, Bradford upon Avon and Doncaster for example, the tourist centre is located in the entrance lobby to the very busy public library. Given the economic importance of all kinds of tourism to local economies – day trips, educational tourism, visiting friends and relatives – public libraries can play an important role "interpreting" the town to outsiders and providing high-quality information about the "local distinctiveness", to adopt a current phrase, of the local community.

But a public library is more than that. It is a different kind of space in the town centre representing an even greater opportunity to embody and celebrate local difference than is still currently appreciated generally.

Libraries and bookshops: shared traditions

Not only does the public library fit naturally into the daily life of many town, city and urban centres, it has often had a strong, direct relationship with local retailing, particularly bookselling. In fact, libraries and bookshops share many traditions. Both have had their own independent and radical traditions, with social, educational and political movements of all kinds establishing their own libraries and bookshops around which to congregate and spread the word. Both have often been important gathering points and homes of new artistic and cultural movements.

For the first half of this century, the Whitechapel Library in East London was the centre of local Jewish cultural life, and the poet Isaac Rosenberg and the painters David Bomberg and Mark Gertler treated it as their home; Rosenberg autographed a copy of his early poems for the librarian Mr Bogdin; another Whitechapel librarian, Morley Dainlow, introduced Rosenberg to the work of a number of Victorian poets as well as writing comments on Rosenberg's own first attempts at poetry.[3] No doubt countless other librarians have performed similarly encouraging roles elsewhere. On several occasions in their paper, Dave Muddiman and Alistair Black point out that, for example, "Though subordinate to library committees, librarians were often civic figures, actively participating in the local community and its moral and cultural organisations."[4]

Many local libraries have acted as small publishing houses for local writers and local historians. For many years, Hackney's library services not only organized an annual poetry competition, but also published an annual anthology of the winning poems. Today, as Keiran Phelan has shown, many libraries organize and play host to public readings, not just by local writers but as part of national literature promotion schemes.

Specialist and independent bookshops have fulfilled similar functions. In the 1920s and 1930s, Harold Munro's Poetry Bookshop in Soho was the hub of the English and American avant-garde poetry scene; today, Bernard Stone's Turret Bookshop in Holborn plays a similar role. Contemporary specialist bookshops such as *Compendium, Silver Moon, The Libertarian Bookshop, Zwemmer's Art Bookshop, Stanford's Map and Travel Bookshop* – all in London admittedly – act as focal points for enthusiasms and interests with which they are associated: advertising meetings, organizing readings and book launches, and taking a much more active role than simply selling books. When the Compendium bookshop recently celebrated its 25th anniversary, it produced a short history of the bookshop, rightly pointing out its enormous influence on British cultural life through its role as a conduit into Britain of American literature and European philosophy, among many other influences. This role was attributed to the enthusiasm and expertise of the staff:

> Throughout the history of Compendium the role of individual members of staff cannot be over-estimated. The policy was always to employ people who were more than specialists in their subject – they were obsessives with an encyclopaedic knowledge of their individual areas. Responsibility for the section meant doing everything – ordering and reordering the books, selling the books, answering telephone enquiries on their subjects, maintaining links with the most obscure of publishers and distributors, keeping completely up to date in their subject both here and in the USA, as well as sweeping, tidying and keeping at bay the overwhelming and volatile groundswell of customers. Endlessly

erudite and operating, particularly at Christmas and holidays, in an atmosphere of barely controlled dementia, the efforts of the staff – many of whom stayed for decades – have always been the most vital component in the success of the shop.[5]

But this has never simply been a London phenomenon. In many small towns and cities, the independently owned bookshop (including the second-hand bookshop) has often been a focal point for local cultural life, putting up posters advertising local events in the window, carrying leaflets for local campaigns, providing a notice-board for voluntary organizations. Most people who choose to own or manage small bookshops, new or second-hand, do not do it primarily for economic gain but because they simply love books. Interestingly, a number of the newer multiples such as Waterstones and Dillons have followed and adopted this personalized, "cultural centre" approach, with programmes of readings, guest signings, late opening hours and notice-boards. A recent study of the early Caribbean Artists Movement in Britain shows how emerging Black British writers such as E. K. Braithwaite, Andrew Salkey and John La Rose met and focused their activities around the New Beacon Bookshop in Finsbury Park, still trading today.[6] Book industry experts predict that the only hope for the independent bookshop in future lies in a high degree of specialization – travel bookshops, cookery bookshops, ethnic minority bookshops – selling both new and second-hand books, and dealing by mail order, import and export sales. The independent *general* bookshop has virtually disappeared, and many towns and cities are the poorer for that.

Lost connections

A real problem is that many of the historic (and local) links between booksellers and librarians have disappeared with the rise of the large national library suppliers. Libraries now rarely buy significant amounts of stock from local booksellers, though with the development of Local Management of Schools (LMS) many schools are now buying direct from local suppliers rather than through centralized purchasing schemes, a pattern that may presage similar changes in the public library sector in future. As the local independent bookshop becomes a thing of the past, the library has often to take on the sole mantle of being the local literary and cultural centre, particularly in the smaller towns and districts.

On the other hand, the rapid growth of chains of quality bookshops throughout many of Britain's towns and cities in the 1980s, mentioned above, has seemed to pose a new threat to the public library, and threatened to displace its role as the "literary" heart of the town or city. These tastefully and expensively fitted-out bookstores, and their enthusiastic and dedicated staff, have espoused the cause of modern literary fiction with a vengeance, making the public library look even more behind the times than ever. There is a real economic problem here. Because as much as the public library may wish to stock multiple copies of the new Martin Amis, Julian Barnes or Jeanette Winterson novel, and have it available to whoever wants it on publication day, it cannot afford to do so in preference to all the other claims on its resources. The market place, however, offers whatever new book you want, on the spot, if you are prepared to pay.

What the market place doesn't guarantee is that it will still be stocking the book 12 months later. As overheads rise and the recession bites deeper, publishing houses have been investing in shorter print runs, with an expectation of profitability and sales within the first year. There is a much smaller "back catalogue" in modern bookselling. This is the function that the public library has to fulfil.

Despite relatively poor wages, the new bookselling chains have also been able to attract a largely graduate staff, who are recruited on the basis of their enthusiasm for books and ideas. One has to ask why such people are not drawn to or do not choose to stay in the better-paid world of the public library service. We have talked to several managers of these bookshops who were previously public librarians, and for them the loss of job security and even a drop in salary has been more than compensated by their freedom to create an individual bookshop style, to take risks, and to enjoy day-to-day decision making, often shared collectively with other staff. In contrast, actual cuts in many library book budgets, and a widening of the public library brief, has meant a relative de-skilling in public libraries. The ratio between a small number of professionally qualified librarians and unqualified library assistants continues to widen.

Forms of co-operation

It is likely therefore that the public library will be unable to "compete" with commercial bookselling in the field of contemporary literary fiction. On the other hand, it could "complement" the bookshop's activities and in doing so help create a wider public literary culture. This is already beginning to happen in a number of reading promotion schemes, which Keiran Phelan has described in great detail.[7] Many of these promotion schemes, aimed to encourage an interest in new fiction or contemporary poetry, are run in conjunction with commercial booksellers, and joint programmes of readings and shared promotional material have helped increase the issues of some titles by as much as 300%. For example, the "Well Worth Reading" campaign in the Southern Arts Board area managed to secure sponsorship from a number of commercial book-suppliers and booksellers, and over several years of development increased issues of selected titles by more than 200%. The "Hereford and Worcester Contemporary Poetry" promotion, carried out between 1990 and 1992, achieved a threefold increase in audiences at poetry readings as well as a 300% increase in book issues of selected poetry titles. The "Now Read On" campaign in Scotland between 1991 and 1993 resulted in a 329% increase in promoted titles.

In the wake of the success of these schemes, the Arts Council has established new funds for supporting literature promotion schemes in public libraries. While these are to be generally welcomed, it is possible to foresee some dangers. An overemphasis on the need to promote "good" literature, and the wish to claim the public library as a kind of literature centre (evident in the Arts Council material), could well begin to destroy the very quality that makes public libraries so successful as popular cultural institutions – their non-judgemental, catholic stock-holding policy, offering something for everybody. A wedge driven between "good" and "bad" literature could fatally weaken the library ethos, and in so doing destroy it as a popular institution.

Borrowing and buying

Time and again we have hoped to demonstrate in this book the unique place that the public library occupies within the local townscape, and within the prevailing commercial and consumer culture. Nowhere is this more evident than in the obvious fact that unlike shops, libraries *lend* cultural goods (sometimes with a small charge) rather than *sell* them. In a sense, they recycle artefacts and other cultural goods (including paintings, toys, as well as books, cassettes, CDs and videos) within the local culture, allowing people to try things out rather than make a once and for all decision to buy. The very name of the original commercial libraries – *circulating* libraries – conveys well this sense of creating a linked cultural network within the local district or town, a different kind of cultural economy.

The relationship between buying and borrowing is worth exploring further, as it links strongly to new concerns for recycling, and for further understanding of what things people could learn to share and re-use rather than buy and eventually throw away. Books were an obvious format for lending rather than buying in the nineteenth century. The price then for a new novel was prohibitively expensive, and commercial and then public libraries were established to share and amortize the original costs among a number of people. After the Second World War, a number of public libraries began picture loan schemes, responding to the new availability of relatively cheap colour reproductions of famous paintings, which, when framed, people might wish to hang up in their home, office or school for a while. Borrowing rather than buying has been especially important for many parents regarding expensive hardbacked illustrated children's story books, which may be read only once or twice before the child wishes to move on to something else, and that have always been a focal point for library use.

Since then, libraries have adapted to new formats and now lend records, tapes, CDs, videos, language courses and study materials, against certain kinds of opposition, both commercial and cultural. They have been accused of distorting the market by taking unfair advantage of their public subsidy. There are some distance-learning companies and correspondence course providers who refuse to allow their materials to be bought by public libraries, as they regard this as undercutting their own market. But as we have seen, there is a strong correlation between buying and borrowing, not only for books but for records too. People who borrow a lot also tend to buy a lot – but they use borrowing as a means of testing out the market and of exploring new tastes. In recent years, other kinds of loan schemes have emerged in many places – particularly associated with welfare schemes or social action projects – for example "toy libraries", to encourage parents to try out different kinds of toys without first buying them, or "tool libraries", where specialist tools are lent out to people who may need them only once in their life and cannot afford or do not wish to buy them. Car hire, plant hire, formal dress hire, for example, are all commercial responses to the demand for one-off use for products that are too expensive to buy.

The public library then represents a very old institution in the high street, but also a very new one. For as notions of sustainability, of recycling, of borrowing or hiring what you really don't need to buy or own become more commonplace, the library acts as a cultural testing ground or laboratory, within the local cultural market place. Of course some people will always wish to own certain kinds of goods – books, records, tools – as "positional goods", which help establish their own cultural identities. Others may wish only ever to borrow these things. Many people will want to do both. The public library underwrites this choice.

The buying power of libraries

Public libraries have always represented enormous buying power, not simply in general terms but in ways that have had a decisive impact on cultural production. Yet they have rarely used this power strategically and in a co-ordinated way. In 1990–1, public libraries in the United Kingdom spent £103 million on books and £7.6 million on audio-visual materials. The Publishers Association estimates that the public sector (including schools, colleges and universities) accounts for a third of the total UK domestic publishing market. It is clear that there are products – books, magazines, audio tapes, videos, records and CDs – for which the public library network is a crucial, possibly decisive buyer, and without which these products would find it hard to exist. These include:
– large print books for the visually impaired
– specialist magazines and journals
– hardback first novels
– hardback crime fiction
– hardback poetry
– children's picture books
– children's reference books
– many adult reference works, encyclopaedias and dictionaries

– literary and musical biographies
– spoken word records
– specialist record labels.

The library's contribution to cultural production is therefore not just in its direct buying power but in its economic underpinning of a variety of specialist products that commercial producers are then able to make available to a wider market.

The impact of public library buying clearly deserves more detailed study. There may be strategic ways in which librarians, library supply companies and publishers could work more closely together in developing specialist series and editions, both for the public sector and the market place.

Market failure: the role of the public library in underwriting cultural diversity

In supporting specialist publishers, small music labels and the educational video market, the library is doing what public cultural policy – through the work of the Arts Council for example – has always been about: funding and in other ways financially underwriting experimentation, innovation and minority interests in various spheres of cultural production, much of which may well become commercially mainstream and self-financing in time. For example, it is well known that the subsidized repertory theatre in Britain has often been the training ground for young actors and actresses who have eventually become considerably commercial successes in television and film, as have many playwrights and script-writers. It has often been pointed out just how phenomenal the "commercial" success of the Royal Court Theatre was in the 1960s, in terms of the size of the public subsidy that theatre got and in terms of the international play-writing and film successes that emerged from that era of seedbed experimentation – *Look back in anger*, *A taste of honey* and so on. Experimental or publicly subsidized theatres such as the Theatre Royal Stratford or the Bush in London, the Glasgow Citizens' Theatre, Theatre Clwyd in Mold, among others, all regularly send successful productions to the West End where they become popular commercial successes. The artists whose work sells in the Cork Street galleries, or decorates book and record covers and influences design and fashion usually are trained at public expenses in art colleges. The small presses publishing poetry and experimental fiction, often grant-aided from public funds, are often the first stepping-stone for young writers and poets who may go on to considerable international commercial glory.

This role, which public cultural policy often underwrites, in supporting the R&D (research and development) function for the wider industry in music, literature, choreography, painting, crafts and other art forms has always been played by the public library network too. For public libraries have often been the primary market for hardback first novels, for poetry, for ethnic minority literature, for literature in translation, for minority interest reference books, journals and magazines, and in doing so have played an important role in sustaining artistic independence, innovation and cultural diversity.

The library as a gatekeeper to the market place

In this final section we look in greater depth at the likely role that the library of the future will play in relation to the commercial market place of cultural production. We have no doubt that the public library will neither be displaced nor superseded by direct home-based consumer culture, but that there will always be a role for the library as a popular testing ground for the acquisition of new tastes, a free source of "speculative" cultural experimentation, which the commercial market may well finally provide, at cost. In this the library continues to fulfil its traditional function which is not as a competitor to the market, or a distorting mechanism or intervention in an otherwise perfect system of supply and demand, but as *a laboratory for choice*. In Working Paper 8, Chris Batt, Director of Croydon's brand-new, state-of-the-art, public library, imagined the library service of 2012 thus:

> Across the country there is still a thriving public library service. Going into the central or the branch libraries of the authority I visited is not a culture shock. There are still shelves of books and people browsing among them. These are the experience hunters who have rejected the widely available alternatives to books as inappropriate for leisure and pleasure reading. The popular areas

for browsing – fiction, biography, some aspects of history are all book based. Looking around at the more technical subjects such as science, computer studies, even gardening, there are still books, but interspersed there are other media to select. CD-ROM is very much in evidence offering a collection of books or manuals in a form that can be accessed from the latest version of the *Bookman*. Rather than borrow six books as customers could in 1993, they can now take a CD-ROM with 50 titles on a subject. These sections themselves are quite small since for many subjects 50 titles is all that are available. The display space is therefore taken up as much with details of what is on the CD-ROM – contents, level, that sort of thing. Interestingly all the informational material is supplied to a national standard by the publisher, although the CD-ROMs are still loaned free. The trick is that the customer can, if they like what they borrow, send a message to the publisher across the national broadband network and they will be supplied with all or any of the titles on the CD-ROM that they wish to purchase, downloaded into their home unit. The information is still freely available from the library, but a sale can be closed if the customer wants to keep the product. The original CD-ROM is returned to the library.[8]

As the prince says in Lampedusa's great novel *The leopard*, in order that things stay the same, everything must change.

CHAPTER 10

The invisible web:
the public library and social policy

Public libraries enshrine the principle of "the right to know" – the right to literacy and the right of access to knowledge. This is not just an intellectual right but a social right as well. It is this principle that helps to make public libraries archetypal buildings and places within British civil society.[1] The right to literacy and to a shared cultural heritage is a clear social principle that is embedded in and supported throughout our society. Indeed, it is the strength and clarity of this ideal that has paradoxically allowed public libraries to be flexible institutions. They have evolved and adapted to meet the needs of people and places. The libraries in Birmingham city centre and in a Lewisham neighbourhood area, for example, are both clearly identifiable as public libraries, and yet each responds to the particular requirements of its location in adaptable and responsive ways.

In the process of evolving and adapting to particular places, public libraries have become part of the fabric of civic society. They are a source of support for many different kinds of activities. Libraries can be a bedrock helping to sustain the life of a locality. They are used by individuals and groups carrying out the day-to-day activity that keeps society going. This is what we have termed the "social impact" of the library. The social impact public libraries have is undervalued and often excluded from assessments of their efficiency and economic value. The purpose of this chapter is to explore the impact that libraries have in communities, and to argue that these effects should be included in exercises designed to measure the performance of public libraries. Policymakers and those concerned with librarianship training might consider ways in which the public library service can build on the best of these by-products of the philosophy of public service in articulating a new social purpose for the public library service.

An entry point to the wider culture

During the course of this century, public libraries have been part of what was defined at the beginning of this book as the public sphere. Public libraries reflect some of these ideals of the civil society and the need to make sure that citizens have access to the basic resources that allow them to enter a public sphere, and literally "belong" to society. The public library provides one of these points of connection between the individual and society. It combines the conceptual principle of the right to literacy and knowledge with the physical rights of access to a building – a public institution. The institutional rules of public libraries are inclusive rather than exclusive. Libraries are non-stigmatizing places. The individual's right of access without having to ask permission or even having to speak to anyone has given libraries an admirably low "entry threshold" compared to most other public institutions.

Their relative openness makes public libraries uniquely accessible places. The library works as an entry point to a wider society for many different groups and it therefore has a particular kind of socializing role. Our study encountered many different ways in which this principle has been translated into practice. The sense of openness and accessibility goes to the heart of the idea of the public sphere.

The symbolic value of the children's library ticket

Children's libraries are one of the few public places parents can take pre-school-age children to. Discussions held with parents in Birmingham found that owning a library ticket is likely to be one of the child's first links to a wider society and one of the first ways of being recognized as an individual citizen.

The potential value of public libraries in introducing children to reading and supporting their education is obvious, and children's librarians form a specialist sector within the profession. What is less well understood is the value of the library as a place that is regularly and uniformly open to children. There are few other institutions to which children have right of access. Our research demonstrated the use children make of public libraries after school and on Saturdays. As well as gathering there to do homework, children in one local library in West London used the library as a place to stop between school and home, as an intermediary zone. The library allowed for an extension of some of the social aspects of the school. Children used the children's library to play board-games, read and talk. The library provides a place that is neither school nor home *and allows children a presence in a public domain in which they are cast neither as potential victims – or as threats*. At a time when the freedom of children is curtailed by fear for their safety and by their lack of personal mobility, a local library can provide social opportunities as well as educational ones. Situated, as it is, outside the school and the home, the library is also symbolic of a wider social and public realm.

The exploitation of children's libraries located in busy shopping areas and their use as surrogate crèches by shoppers shows just how limited facilities for children are in shopping areas (and in city centres generally). In Birmingham, it is the library service that has led to the development of plans for the new "Centre of the Child" in the city centre, a dedicated space for children's activities – a home in the heart of the city.

A window on the world

Most libraries provide newspapers and magazines. In fact the reading room or newsroom has always been a part of that civic philosophy to provide and give access to the news and information that helps to form public opinion, so essential to the public realm. Robert Snape suggests that the provision of newsrooms was a legacy of the mechanics' institutes. Newsrooms provided reference reading – newspapers and magazines. They were both social places and provided the means for individuals to take part in a wider social and political debate. The provision of newsrooms is also a legacy of the liberalizing "coffee house" tradition that helped to influence the establishment of public libraries.[2]

The provision of newspapers and magazines is still a popular function of public libraries, particularly for men. The research undertaken for the purposes of the Comedia study showed both a high use of newspapers and the way their provision in libraries has been adapted to meet new needs. For example, a small library in Hounslow with a substantial Asian population provides a unique kind of news service. The library supplies a mixture of English and Asian newspapers providing a specialist current affairs perspective that begins to match the social and cultural interests of readers.

Going to a library to read newspapers is one of the uses that requires least contact with the mechanics of the institution. There is no need to approach staff, no need for a ticket, no need for membership or to have items stamped when entering or leaving. No need, either, to speak the same language, for many of the newspapers kept in libraries are in other languages.

Libraries often stock a range of papers and magazines that particular individuals or groups may not like on moral or religious grounds. However, libraries still have a powerful secular brief to provide for a general interest. Such a brief does not provide watertight guidelines and there is perpetual debate amongst library staff and the profession generally about what to include and to reject. Once accepted on the library shelves, however, newspapers and magazines are generally respected as part of a regime designed to serve a general interest. The claim to a larger neutrality is also reflected in the public library service in Northern Ireland which has always been one of the few areas of neutral public territory in a society sharply divided along religious and sectarian lines.

Some libraries have experimented with television sets (with earphones), offering an opportunity to watch educational, local history and other videos *in situ*: Dublin Central Library has a bank of them and they are well used. No doubt soon, some libraries will be installing satellite television, enabling people to watch (in silence) news from around the world and in other languages.

A civic centre

The neutrality of the library and the claim to serve the higher sphere of general interest establishes public libraries as safe and legitimate places for most people. Public libraries create non-discriminating spaces for people to be. Discussions with women who worked in Birmingham city centre showed that along with the museum and art gallery, the public library is a place that is easy and "comfortable" to visit alone. Unlike some other social facilities available in the city centre, whether public or commercial, the library presents few barriers or threats to a sense of personal ease and comfort. The library is a place where people feel relatively safe in public. The case studies in Hounslow and Birmingham showed the library to be an important social and study place for Asian teenagers for whom the city centre library represented a safe and respectable environment.

The library and wider questions of cultural diversity

The public library has a long history of being an entry point into the wider society for Britain's ethnic minorities. Starting with an aim to provide materials for those whose cultural origins were not English, it is now – as are other public institutions – faced with the task of reflecting a society that has become increasingly heterogeneous in its allegiances and roots.

In a history of response, some of the key moments have been:
- After the Second World War whose aftermath brought a number of strong communities to Britain – German Jews, Poles, Ukrainians, Serbs, Romanians, refugees from the Baltic states of Lithuania, Latvia and Estonia. Setting up their own organizations for themselves, particularly (where eastern Europeans were concerned) in the northern mill towns, they presented a coherence and articulacy that resulted in a measure of official public library response. Libraries began to stock books in the mother tongues of the new Britons.
- When new immigrants started to enter from Asia, the first response was to follow the pattern already established for European immigrants. Ethnic librarians (a new invention) began to acquire books in the languages of countries of origin. This was not an easy task: books were often hard to obtain, costly and less sturdy than necessary for library use. Moreover, it began to emerge, Asian immigrants were, particularly in the early stages, from rural areas: they had little tradition of leisure reading.
- The growth area where Asian communities were concerned proved not so much books as non-English magazines and newspapers, as

the Hounslow case study demonstrated. These sometimes come from the countries of origin, but not always. Britain still abounds with "language" publications – *Daily Jang* (Urdu), *Garavi Gujarat* (Gujarati), *Bengali Samachar* (Bengali), *Des Pardes* (Punjabi) and others. Language and culture are life-lines. They do not in themselves represent a rejection of being British, rather a recognition that being British now represents a wider variety of possibilities than it did fifty years ago. For libraries, the attitude towards the retention of language is more complex than it seems.

– The mother tongue movement has kept the issue well to the fore, backed up by the production of attractive dual-language books and tapes.
– The lines of communication are kept open (and for the population at large) by other means. The development of an oral culture has been one of the strengths of recent years, and one to which libraries have contributed, through the provision of tapes and other materials.
– Libraries have also been sponsors, although less spectacularly, to Black and Asian writing. The difficulties of translation have led to its being a relatively closed tradition hitherto. However, new technology has opened out the possibility of translation. The Arts Council-sponsored series of Asian works in English in the autumn of 1993 has helped to open up the field to non-Asian readers.
– Libraries have a part to play in translation and dissemination, an extension of their function as platforms for new reading and publications. They have launched new community-based work at their branches in the past; they still act as bases for readings and tours.

Such surveys into ethnic minority use of libraries, for example one undertaken by Haringey Council Community Services Committee in 1990, showed that – with 41% of respondents to library questionnaires coming from "black and minority ethnic communities" – "library usage in general reflects the composition of Haringey's population very closely and that libraries are therefore used by a wide cross-section of the community".[3] A good example of the lengths to which libraries have gone, not only to meet the literary interests of ethnic minority groups, but also to celebrate the contribution of other literatures to what has traditionally been a rather insular "English canon", has been the work of Lambeth Library Services. In recent years Lambeth have published an excellent series of attractively designed brochures and guides, including, *Novelists from the Indian sub-continent: a selection of writing in English*,

Ireland: an introduction to books available from Lambeth libraries, *Black men writers: fiction from Africa and the Caribbean*, *Black poetry* and *Black women writers: an introduction.* All these provide a starting point or gateway into a new body of work and writing.

The library as passport

Though ethnic minorities come to libraries for the functions outlined above – for books, periodicals, readings and so on – the significance of the public library goes beyond all these. As with many other things, it is greater than the sum of its parts. *The library, in essence, acts as an entry point to the wider, multicultural and cosmopolitan British life.*

At a simple level it represents respectability. Both Birmingham and Hounslow Central Library are particularly aware of this. Their large spaces are heavily used by young Asians to socialize as well as to study. The library is an approved space in Asian family terms. It is acceptable (even desirable) for young girls, who often come from more tightly controlled backgrounds than their white counterparts, to go off to the library for the day.

The library is also a source of information. As Birmingham library's own research shows, it is well used by local black people looking for material to assist voluntary organizations. The library has helped in the development of Saturday schools and community self-help ventures. The designs for Notting Hill's massive carnival frequently have had their genesis in local public libraries around London.

The neighbourhood library and the network of caring

The role of local libraries in supporting the social infrastructure of their surrounding community is relatively under-researched. However, case-study work began to show how, in areas of multiple deprivation, local libraries were used by those members of the community who were active in sustaining the community. In supporting the emotional needs of particular groups in the community – the carers, the activists and the volunteers – *the library was supporting some of the most strategically important people in the community who help to provide stability and continuity.* Whereas many public agencies working in disadvantaged areas are funded to offset or diminish the negative aspects of community life – unemployment, youth disaffection, alcohol and drug problems, family breakup – the public library supports the positive. In one case-study area – an estate in Middlesbrough – it was clear that the library was the only building that was not marked out as a symbol of welfare, compensation and deprivation. Instead, the library was an affirmative public institution linking the locality to a wider public sphere.

These examples illustrate some of the ways in which public libraries recognize people as individuals and as citizens. Our argument here is that the social impact of libraries stems from the way they inform a sense of the public domain that is open to all. They give shape and identity to a notion of society, even if some politicians have doubted whether such a thing as society even exists.

Caring and sharing

Public libraries help to support other areas of the social infrastructure. They provide resources for the more formal social services, such as supplying hospitals and old people's homes with mobile library services. Libraries also run home visits and supply books to people who are housebound. In the Thorntree Library in Middlesbrough, for example, the librarians knew each of their housebound users by first name, knew their taste in books, and kept a close record of all past borrowings so that they could ensure that the book selection they took round was always offering something relevant and new. This was a form of what the market researchers might wish to term "niche marketing" or "strategic targeting" but done in this case with a sense of personalized public service rather than economic reward.

The role public libraries play in supporting carers is not well documented. However, research by the National Federation of Women's Institutes on the work of carers shows the essential although often invisible work carers do and the extent to which the formal health services rely on such work. It is estimated there are some 6.8 million adults responsible for caring for sick, handicapped or elderly people, of whom 1.4 million spend at least 20 hours a week providing care and assistance.[4] Public libraries help to supply information and support carer networks. The ways in which the library network sustains these infrastructures of caring is just one example. Libraries support many of these kinds of social networks upon which society not only depends but through which it is in many ways constituted. As the role of voluntary caring resurfaces in societies that no longer have the resources necessary to underpin all welfare tasks – a fact now acknowledged by political parties of all persuasions – the case for the positive role that the public library plays in voluntary life gains credence all the while.

Libraries have also had to respond to the government's much criticized "Care in the Community" initiative, established with the laudable aim of de-institutionalizing mental patients but with, in many cases, inadequate resources and structures to meet the resulting demands upon community institutions. For it is the public library that has provided a shelter or safe haven for many people unused to coping – and without the means to do so – within the busy and indifferent world of the modern town or city.

Linked to these questions of caring and sharing is the related value of the act of reading itself, which can provide mental space and freedom from immediate demands and pressures. For elderly people living alone, the visit from the librarian and a supply of books can help to sustain mental health. Our survey work and interviews revealed that the reading habit was a central and psychologically important part of the heavy library user's daily life. At a time when mental health problems – particularly depression – are shown to be widespread, the role of the public library in supporting these general emotional needs should not be dismissed.[5]

Measuring the intangibles

Clearly, it is important and necessary constantly to assess the performance of public libraries but there is a danger of measuring only those things that are easy to measure – book issues, and attendances – and to disregard the positive social effects a library can have on its locality. As the competitions and awards for community initiatives show, local libraries often help to pioneer imaginative community projects. In Cleveland, the Annexe Library in Hartlepool offers cookery classes, advice for small businesses, help with a community newspaper, and even supplies sewing machines.

Cheaper than policemen?

The Cleveland survey suggested that it might well be possible to develop indicators of the more qualitative kind, both in terms of individual self-development or collective social benefit. But this in turn raises the question of whether a price can be put on such a service – particularly in an increasingly market-driven society. We know that on average the public library service costs £12 per head per person per annum, and that each book issue costs perhaps £1, or slightly more. But how do you put a price on the benefits a library might bring to a demoralized community? Ironically, the answer may reside in one of the founding arguments for the public libraries themselves in 1850 when, during the parliamentary debate, one MP argued that "libraries are cheaper than policemen". Perhaps we have come full circle, 150 years later, and indeed have to argue that a neighbourhood library is cheaper than half a dozen anti-crime projects, custodial sentences on young offenders, or individuals institutionalized as a result of family breakdown. For it is certainly the case that there are many difficult areas in Britain where the public library is the last affirmative, dignifying and respected public institution, among many others whose function it is – more negatively – to redress social problems, to repair social damage or to counterbalance social disintegration. Deprivation is fairly easy to quantify, but how do you measure community spirit?

To discuss libraries in this way is to talk about economic and social impacts, cost-benefit analysis and economic externalities. The case against the public subsidy of libraries has been put by Laurence White:

> On close examination, the case for a tax-supported library that provides services to users at zero cost is not a strong one. The strongest arguments are for those public-library services for children and students; the educational benefits of these services appear to provide adequate justification. The case is much weaker for adult services. Actual use patterns will not support educational or income-distribution arguments. The positive externalities from adult use are not substantial or pervasive.[6]

But the Cleveland case study suggested – and obviously much more detailed work is needed – that the cost of maintaining a public library in areas of multiple social disadvantage, *compared to the costs of not supporting the library* (in terms of further community breakdown, social anomy and increased welfare provision), is an economic and social benefit in the wider sense. It could be argued that the externalities of social cohesion are a valid argument for the public support of adult services in many areas, and that, crudely, the neighbourhood library is a much cheaper form of welfare provision than the alternative costs of increased policing, custody costs and other factors. This case is strengthened by the fact that it is to two of the most vulnerable groups in the community – children and the elderly – that the public library has traditionally been most responsive, the two who statistically are among its most frequent users.

The case is certainly not proven, and much more empirical work is needed. But we are convinced that the community library has a strategic and enabling part to play in the repertoire of an holistic community development approach, among so many compensatory, welfarist or crime prevention strategies. Perhaps it is now time for the public library movement to initiate more quantifiable research on the economic and social impact of the public library.

CHAPTER 11

Education and life-long learning

The idea of a learning society offers a broad vision. It rejects privilege – the idea that it is right for birth to determine destiny. It transcends the principle of meritocracy, which selects for advancement only those judged worthy and rejects as failures those who are not. A learning society would be one in which everybody participated in education and training (formal and informal) throughout their life. It would be a society characterised by high standards and low failure rates. In the past we have too often allowed ourselves to believe that high standards can only be achieved at the expense of high rates of failure; or that low levels of failure necessarily entail low standards. In the learning society this would not be the case.

(*Learning pays*, Royal Society for the Arts, April 1991)

The last decade has seen enormous changes in education provision, management and delivery in Britain. The 1988 Education Act, introducing local management into schools, and the detaching of schools from local authority control, had a major impact on public libraries, as has also the rapid expansion of further and higher education in the same period. As Sir Christopher Ball noted in his paper "The learning society", "participation in higher education has risen from 1 in 8 to 1 in 5 between 1979 and 1991 (the target is 1 in 3 by the year 2000)".[1] Yet even so, this picture of expansion pales besides figures from other countries. Statistics provided by the National Institute of Economic and Social Research reveal that, in comparison with France, Germany and Japan, Britain fares as shown in Table 11.1.[2]

Table 11.1   Comparative educational attainment.

	16-yr-olds with GCSE equivalents	18+ with HE entry requirements	16–19-yr-olds in education/ training
Britain	27%	29%	56%
France	66%	48%	76%
Germany	62%	68%	79%
Japan	50%	80%	94%

Source: National Institute of Economic and Social Research (1993).

South Korea's target is 80% university entrance level students by the year 2000 – Britain's is 30%. Britain also fares badly in comparison with many other countries in the proportion of the educational budget devoted to nursery schools: 4% in Britain, but 11% in Norway, and 10% in France.[3] The rediscovery of the issue of adult literacy in the 1970s – estimates in June 1993 assumed a UK population of people lacking functional literacy at 6 million – also reveals the problems to be tackled at the other end of the educational spectrum. Yet society is going to get more complicated and more demanding of personal and intellectual skills: it is worth noting that it is estimated that the sum total of current human knowledge will comprise only 1% of what is known in the year 2050.[4]

The implications of these trends are enormous. It is already clear, for example, that education – or perhaps it is better to use the word learning – is bursting the banks of institutional provision, and is happening increasingly away from the formal schools and colleges. Developments in information and communications technologies "have succeeded in divorcing knowledge from institutions".[5] The Open University was a pioneer in this trend, allowing students to work from home, often at times most convenient to themselves, using a mixture of set books, radio and television programmes, together with the occasional face to face seminar and participatory summer school. What was particularly important about this development was that in breaking out of the institutional boundaries, and using the popular media of broadcasting and publishing, many other people were able to "eavesdrop" in on these courses and programmes, without needing to register or take exams. The Open University, which has become Britain's largest single teaching institution, had 210,000 people studying with it in 1993. It has also educated many more people than those registered, and it is this *porosity* of the new educational forms that is one of their distinguishing features. It is worth noting that recently the Open University has begun to advertise "Leisure Packs" in the national press, offering study packs and courses for those who simply want to find out more about a subject, but don't necessarily wish to enrol on a course or gain qualifications. In the modern world of mass publishing and broadcasting, people are educating themselves all the time.

The massive expansion of higher education through the rise of the polytechnics in the 1970s and 1980s was not simply a matter of numbers but also involved a change of style and format. Students were increasingly encouraged to study across disciplines, or to develop their own degree course based on modules chosen from a variety of subjects. The age group taking degrees changed, as did the traditional notion of going away from home for three years to study for a degree. For example, there has been a growth of part-time adult courses run in universities. The University of Exeter has more than 5,000 part-time students in 300 study programmes. Warwick has 1,500 students enrolled in part-time postgraduate courses taught by modular and distance-learning networks. Higher education has become more like a part of daily life for many people: they study locally, and they still live at home, often carrying on bringing up families and staying involved in local life. Similarly the polytechnics broke down the barrier between "vocational" and "non-vocational" education, with many courses explicitly geared to professional qualifications and opportunities: degrees in social work, in education, in archaeology and so on.

What Britain and the rest of the world are witnessing and living through is the dissolution of the traditional boundaries between "education" and "life", or between what the historian E. P. Thompson once characterized as "customary" and "educated" experience, as well as those between vocational and non-vocational forms of knowledge. In a technology-based, complex society, in which knowledge changes every year, people are going to have to consider education not as a once and for all opportunity that some get and others don't, but as something that everybody will need access to for the whole of their life. Hence the notion of "the learning society" and hence the enormous implications for public and private institutions of all kinds. For example, it is already becoming a matter of custom to refer to "the learning company", one which sees the continuing skills' upgrading and educational development of its employees as a matter not just of moral probity – but perhaps more importantly – of competitive advantage. At Ford UK, all employees receive a grant for non-job-related education and training, and the Nissan Company has its own Open Learning Centre, as does Rolls Royce.[6]

These trends should be familiar to librarians, for in many ways the wheel has come full circle, and the public library is regaining its educational role within the wider society. For the public library movement grew out of the early nineteenth-century mechanics' institutes – among a number of originating influences – which were dedicated to the self-improvement and education of ordinary working-class people denied access to formal education. The provision of a library was a central feature of these institutes. By the middle of the nineteenth century there were some 700 such institutes in Britain, the largest of which, for example, Manchester Mechanics Institute, had a library of 12,000 volumes in 1850.[7] In many places the establishment of the public library out of local rates had to be agreed by a poll of ratepayers, and it was usually the educational argument (rather than a more general cultural argument) that won the case. The contrast of the library with the public house was made everywhere, with, for example, the *Middlesex Courier* arguing that "The public house is the ante-room of the gaol, while the library is the doorway of the knowledge which is power – power for success, for prosperity, and for honour. The public house is the high road to perdition; the library the wicket of truth."[8] What is particularly interesting about this description is that the library is described as a doorway or a wicket, with the implication that librarians are gatekeepers to knowledge, rather than direct providers themselves. This is once again thoroughly modern.

Learning about learning

If the trend is towards individuals taking on responsibility for their own learning programmes throughout their lives, then the emphasis moves away from the passive recipient of knowledge based in an educational institution (the worst of the traditional classroom model) to the active learner finding out about things from a variety of sources, only some of which will remain classes and courses based in specialized buildings. The move, in fact, from a model of education-based teaching to one based on learning. A good example of this issue is raised by the debate about children's reading skills. Although it remains unclear whether reading standards have declined, one expert has drawn attention to the problem of "independent" reading. John Bald, who has carried out research into reading standards in Essex, has argued that: "The breadth of reading in schools has increased, and that is good, but it has been done at the expense of ensuring that children can read text independently."[9]

It is the public library or the school library that supports independent reading, a skill and a competence that should be valued differently to that of instrumental reading.

What psychologists of learning are now saying is that the most important skill of all in this model is not rooted in the acquisition of knowledge, or in the subject matter itself, but in the motivating and self-rewarding quality of *learning to learn*.[10] This quality combines a mixture of study skills, reading skills, interpretative skills, and an awareness of the processes and sources of new information and knowledge in a deregulated and de-institutionalized world. Who better to acquaint people with these skills than librarians?

One of the results of these trends is that education takes on more of the characteristics of leisure – particularly of the personal self-development kind – in many of its forms and aptitudes. For *in modern societies the onus of educational development and skills enhancement is increasingly placed upon the individual rather than the employer*, since most people will change the number and nature of their employers many times in the course of their working life. This is an issue of intellectual and institutional location that affects public libraries directly, as do all these trends of course. These issues can be presented in a more schematic way. If the two dominant paradigms for the encouragement of, and provision for, personal and intellectual development are still "education" and "leisure", what follows is a taxonomy of traditions, skills and assumptions that appear to belong to each one. They are of course not watertight and wholly separate lists. Nevertheless, identifying the education and leisure paradigms as the two main frameworks for future strategy and presenting them in a schematic way (see Table 11.2) may help clarify some of the more difficult philosophical, strategic and managerial decisions that lie ahead: particularly for librarians.

Even drawing up this list helps clarify the fact that even though the origins of the public libraries lie in a kind of educational imperative, it has always been wholly voluntary and wholly self-defined. What brought these issues suddenly to the fore, certainly in the course of the

Table 11.2   A tale of two paradigms.

The educational paradigm	The leisure paradigm
Compulsory	Voluntary
Teaching	Learning
Back to basics	The shock of the new
Collective	Individual
Civil society	The open market
Local management of schools	Commercialization
Producer-led	Consumer-led
National curriculum	Citizen's Charter
Streamed	Unstreamed
Sectarian/religious	Secular
Success and failure	Individual development
Tested	Validated
Hierarchies of knowledge	Pick and mix
Hierarchies of transmission	Autodidactic
Ordered by age	Lifelong
Building-based	Home-community-based
Institutional space	Public realm
Instrumental knowledge	Self-expression

Comedia study, was the rapid rise of open learning modes at all levels in all kinds of institutions, whether educational, library, home, business or workplace, and *the dependence of the open learning mode on the skills of the librarian rather than the skills of the teacher*. But these are not mechanical, instrumental skills, however. It is not enough for the librarian to be able to show someone how to access a database or understand the Dewey decimal system. For as Professor Robin Alston has argued, in advising caution against the notion that computers will solve all of the problems faced by librarians, no idea is "more malign, I think, than the notion that knowledge is amenable to mechanical transference. *Information* without doubt, but *knowledge* decidedly not."[11]

This issue was highlighted in the national study as a result of a small discussion group held at the ULIDIA Centre in Belfast in which a mixed group of teachers and librarians were asked by one of the Comedia team to state whether they thought that teachers and librarians were intellectual peers. It was clear that this was an area of considerable ambiguity on both sides. It seemed that some teachers regard librarians as technicians, whose bibliographical skills and knowledge of resources was an "add-on" to the traditional educational skill of curriculum development and syllabus writing. Yet it can be argued that in today's complex societies, bibliographical and information access skills are central to all educational programmes, and that librarians have to be in at the beginning.

The skills as yet still underdeveloped within librarianship are precisely those that enable them to transform information into knowledge. And this quintessentially is the skill of *interpretation*. When interviewed as part of the Comedia study, Michael Assor, Director of Leisure and Arts at Oxford County Council, was asked how the library service had fitted into the larger corporate leisure department. For the most part, very well he thought. But the librarians had learned a lot very quickly from working more closely with colleagues in the museum world, principally in the value that museum staff now place, not so much on their curatorial role but on that of interpretation. This was a professional, cultural and intellectual shift that still has to be made within librarianship.

Open learning: a vision of the future?

It really has been the sudden and rapid expansion of open learning schemes that has brought these latent dichotomies out into the open. Even bearing in mind the qualification that open learning may be just a fad, an attractive but fundamentally flawed form of education and training, the issues raised by computer-based, individualized forms of learning will not go away. Open learning has been defined by P. G. Cleary in the Library and Information Plan for Northern Ireland as "a form of flexible education and training service which puts the needs of the consumer of that service before the requirements of its provider". In the words of a recent Department of Employment study:

> Open learning requires people to take responsibility for their learning – they have to be active in organising their learning and seeking help and information. At the same time it puts the learner at centre stage – the emphasis is on the learner learning, not the learner being taught.[12]

In brief, open learning starts with the individual's wants and needs and develops a tailor-made package of training and education around those needs. It has clearly developed in an era of rapid technological and industrial change, in which employment skills have to be constantly updated and renewed. It is largely aimed at unemployed people, or people wishing to gain new vocational skills, and can be the first step on the rung to new career opportunities. The voluntary nature of open learning, the fact that the responsibility for the process is in the hands of the learner, suggests many parallels with the origins and contemporary ethos of the public library service, which is autodidactic, self-rewarding and largely informal. Parallels are suggested also between the "browsing" culture of library use and the self-selecting quality of open learning materials, which encourage the user to dip in and out of different programmes and units as appropriate.

Yet some qualifications need to be made. In a deregulated, highly casualized and small business environment, there may be an increasing crossover between traditional "vocational" skills and what have previously been regarded as hobby interests or leisure pursuits. Indeed, the National Institute for Adult Education is currently in dispute with HM Customs and Excise over the levying of VAT on "leisure" as opposed to "vocational" adult classes, as if it were possible to draw a sharp distinction between the two.[13] Embroidery is both a hobby and a vocational skill; so are cake-decorating, car maintenance, kite-making, photography, lettering and design. The fixed barriers and dividing lines between vocational and non-vocational subjects and skills are breaking down. Open learning is highly suited to these changes.

Open learning, therefore, is an educational process *but which shares most of the characteristics of the leisure paradigm.* It is voluntary, access-based, consumer-led, highly individualized, unstreamed and life-long. It is, in short, like going to the library used to be – and for many still is. There are outstanding problems – of validation, of quality control of materials, of the range of learning packages available. But these issues are now being tackled.

The long-term implications of this connection between public libraries and new technology-based personalized learning need to be dealt with more fully. But some key points are worth making here.

- The first is the sheer scale of the "life-long learning" revolution. Currently more than 6 million UK adults are involved in some kind of education every week (not including distance learning, library-based open learning schemes, and that provided by voluntary organizations).

- The second point is the breakdown, already mentioned, between vocational and non-vocational skills in a world in which home-based or technology-based employment is growing. The enormous success in take-up of the new General National Vocational Qualifications (GNVQs), the vocational equivalent of A-levels launched in 1992, attests to the demand for vocational education.
- The third issue is that in accommodating these new forms of personalized learning, which require the active role of the learner in creating his or her own learning package, the public library is returning to some of its original traditions in supporting the active self-educator.
- Fourthly, that in these new learning forms, the skills of the librarian are more appropriate and valued than the traditional skills of the teacher.

In the London borough of Lewisham, where the case study on evaluating the success of open learning schemes in libraries was based, it is clear that the public library offers many advantages as a base for such schemes. Many students we interviewed felt "at home" in the library, coming to use the packages to fit in with their own work or domestic timetables, and without what they regarded as the bureaucracy of formal education. There were high percentages of women and ethnic minority students using the schemes, overcoming some of the obstacles that more traditional forms of education encounter in widening their student base. These are some of the comments that were made:

> Tried an evening class but terrified of computers . . . the best thing about doing sessions in the library is being left alone to get on with it at your own pace.   (Middle-aged woman)

> The staff here have worked out a syllabus for the IT element I'm doing for a sports leader award . . . the advantage of this scheme is I can fit it around other things like looking for a job.
> (Male unemployed)

> Always been a library member but never been to evening classes . . . made redundant last year and using word processing packages to keep my hand in and improve typing speed.
> (Middle-aged, Afro-Caribbean woman, unemployed)

I could have learnt computer skills at university but didn't want someone standing over me telling me what to do . . . found out about it from a friend and now sometimes use library as well.

(Afro-Caribbean, full-time PhD student)

It was acknowledged that library-based schemes (as they are currently set up) could only take students so far. Librarians are not trained to award qualifications, or assess educational development, but as a starting point on the educational ladder, it is clear to us that public libraries have found a dynamic new role to play. This also appears to be the view of the Department of Employment and other training and educational agencies. David Hough, national programme organizer of the Department of Employment "Open for Learning" scheme in public libraries, has stated that "Libraries are open to everyone and it is easy to go along, see what's on offer, and get involved."[14]

Homework centres

The two libraries studied in the Hounslow case study – one a small branch library, the other a larger town centre library – were both used heavily by school and college students as places to study. The increase in project work and the cost of books were given as reasons for studying in the library. But perhaps one of the main reasons for studying in the library was the opportunity to study with friends.

Secondary-school-age children also used the branch library on their journey between school and home to research homework assignments. Between 3.30pm and 5.00pm the library was very busy with school students. Older students tended to make use of the late evening opening hours. They also used the town centre library as an alternative "common room", preferring to spend free periods in the library rather than at school. At certain times of the year the town library, or at least the areas within it designated for quiet reading, are dominated by student use.

For several years now, The Prince's Trust has been engaged in research on study support centres. The Trust has, in many instances in partnership with local authorities, set up 30 pilot study support centres. Research has shown the need for places for out-of-school study and the potential for such centres to improve students' self-confidence and develop independent learning skills. Although most of these are in schools or community centres, there is some crossover between informal use of libraries as homework places and the role of study centres.

It is very likely that the expansion of student numbers in Britain will continue to exert major pressures on public libraries for study spaces, reference books and other materials; and on staff for advice or help with project work.

Skills exchanges

The growth of more flexible forms of education and training parallels greater flexibility in employment practices and local economies. One of the more interesting developments in local economies in areas of high unemployment has been the rise of Local Employment and Trading Schemes (LETS). They are local networks of barter schemes whereby people trade skills, and in doing so develop local "currencies" as a means of formalizing contracts without money changing hands. There are now more than 200 schemes in Britain, and even a national network, Letslink UK, which in 1993 handled 27,000 enquiries. Many schemes have even issued their own chequebooks.

The idea is a development of earlier models of skills exchanges, which were popular in the USA in the 1960s as part of the "alternative culture". The recession in Britain has given them a new boost, and it could be an area in which the public library and its new technology could play a vital community role as an information bank of local skills. A number of economists and local development agencies are looking at the potential of LETS schemes for utilizing what are at present many wasted skills in many communities. Again the public library movement could take the initiative in this field by making contacts with such schemes and adopting a positive role towards using the library as the centre of such networks.

The open library?

It is clear then that the library service already plays a major role in supporting education. Yet this is happening by default, and the problem (or opportunity?) is growing. The library profession, in partnership with educational professionals, needs urgently to clarify its educational purposes and articulate these on a wider stage. But this raises the question as to whether librarianship training, or indeed the professional and staffing structures of public libraries, is adequate to meet these new demands. The question of the new skills needed for librarianship is raised elsewhere, but some points should be made here. One of the most pressing ones is what one might call the "de-skilling" of public libraries, particularly when compared with the world of commercial bookselling. The proportion of (unqualified) library assistants to professionally qualified librarians is increasing. In contrast, and a phenomenon quite rare in contemporary retailing, bookselling is being re-skilled, with several of the national chains now insisting on an all-graduate entry policy. Currently, the most common public complaint about libraries – at least with regard to fiction – is that they are losing out to bookshops, where staff are more informed. "Ten years ago, 37–39 per cent of people were getting their books from libraries first. This new figure (30%) is a huge drop. It is happening because libraries, in spite of their best efforts, are giving much poorer service than bookshops."[15]

If the public library is to reinvent itself as a learning institution – the open library – then librarianship skills and staffing structures will need to be radically reformed. For as the Open School – a sister organization to the Open University and the Open College – has realized, technology alone cannot "solve" the new educational demand and:

> IT cannot solve everything: the human dimension of professional support and encouragement will continue to be necessary to sustain students' faltering progress. A central part of Open School's agenda is therefore to boost teachers' skills, as well as examining the potential for greater use of teaching assistants, student team working arrangements and volunteer distance mentors.[16]

Does the public library profession have these new kinds of attitude towards staff skills enhancement in place, or plans for new kinds of flexible staffing and support services?

CHAPTER 12

Information and the right to know

Now information is starting to redefine our world, its geography and its economy. What would the world look like if information was money? And who would be running it?

(BBC TV, *Horizon*, June 1993)

Libraries and information

Since the 1970s, libraries have identified themselves – sometimes exclusively – with information provision. It has become almost automatic now when describing library services, library training schemes and library policy in general to link the two. In some cases, "information services" now takes precedence over "library services". But what kind of information do libraries provide, how much and to whom? Is it really the core activity of the public library service in contemporary society?

We undertook a survey in conjunction with the library service in Reigate and Redhill on the amount of information being dispensed in the area by the library's County Information Service and by other information providers. Using only those figures provided by organizations who felt able to estimate their weekly rate of enquiry, it was clear that there was an absolute minimum of 3,000 information enquiries within Reigate and Redhill each week. These enquiries covered a broad range of topics. Of those organizations surveyed:

– 60% provided information concerned with employment, including

careers advice and information and advice about training
- 55% provided information relating to children. This ranged from advice about eligibility for benefits to information about recreational activities
- 50% provided advice relating to legal matters
- 50% provided advice relating to education
- 45% dealt with complaints. These ranged from consumer complaints to grievances about statutory services
- 45% dealt with issues relating to the environment
- 40% dealt with enquiries relating to planning and development
- 40% dealt with enquiries relating to welfare and benefits (in addition to those enquiries noted above relating to child benefits).

The number of enquiries monitored was almost certainly a considerable underestimation, since many smaller organizations kept no records of the amount of enquiries with which they assisted. The real figure could well be at least double that. It may well be, therefore, that the various statutory and voluntary agencies within Reigate and Redhill are dealing with a minimum of 6,000 information enquiries each week. There is no reason to suppose that Reigate is at all atypical in the amount of enquiries that its population generates.

The library service's own records show that enquiries are increasing significantly each year. They show, too, that the public library has a particular role within the town's information network. Libraries are still perceived as places where general enquiries can be made, without enquirers leaving themselves vulnerable. Library staff have a brief to help whatever the query. They are not expected to know the answer but they are relied upon to know how to find an answer. Librarians were perceived as neutral by users surveyed in Reigate, unlike those employed to give advice for Council departments. The only other organization with a similar profile was the Citizens' Advice Bureau. A librarian told us that people often brought sensitive documents – birth certificates, immigration papers – to photocopy at the library rather than take them to a commercial photocopy shop that may have been nearer. Librarians are trusted for their reassuring neutrality.

Many people using the library information services found out about them when they were using the library for another purpose. The library, then, still occupies a generalist position in the information network. It is still seen as a place where people expect to be able to find things out, and where they expect the librarians to be able to assist them.

Some libraries have responded to the increasing demand for information by greatly expanding the traditional enquiry desk, and training librarians as information workers, able to assist people to define their requirements clearly, and then helping them satisfy those requirements. Some, like West Surrey, have established fully fledged County Information Services. More are considering doing so.

Librarians and information technology

To date, technological innovation within libraries has largely been "behind the scenes": helping librarians catalogue, access and record more efficiently. Chris Batt notes that the penetration of library management systems across the 167 library authorities in the United Kingdom increased rapidly, from 87 in 1983 to 93 in 1985 and 101 in 1987, reaching 113 in 1989 and 129 in 1991.

Batt calls this a "secondary" benefit of information technology, as far as library users are concerned. But "primary" uses are now becoming much more common, as Table 12.1 shows.[1]

Libraries are just about keeping up with the technology of conventional information provision, and are providing a service for community use. Given the increasing complexity of society, its rules and regulations, its rights and responsibilities, libraries have staked their claim to the provision of information in the name of citizens' rights.

The culture of citizenship and the right to know

The library's response to the increasing demand for information fits in with the wider culture of citizenship – of Citizens' Charters – and the wider principle of "the right to know". One librarian told us that twenty years ago the typical information enquiry concerned train timetables; today it is more likely to be a question about unemployment benefits or legal advice – as the Surrey study demonstrated. In a post-industrial society with new employment and unemployment patterns, financial rights and entitlements gain in importance. Information – at all levels of society – takes on a financial value. An efficient and informed library

Table 12.1 IT in libraries.

Primary use of IT	Total in 1991
On-line access to remote host	107
Private viewdata	40
Automated community information	97
Micros for public use	59
CD-ROM databases	101

service can be dispensing tens of thousands of pounds' worth of information over the counter daily – in terms of benefit entitlements, information about educational grants, business information and so on. But in doing so it is entering a competitive market. It is also entering an area where a recipient of the "wrong" advice may seek redress against the person providing it; hence questions of professional indemnity are now being raised among librarians.

Historically, the state was the key provider of information. Private organizations "controlled" far less information. However, as more developed economies have exported manufacturing to low-cost labour regions, service industries and particularly private information providers have expanded dramatically. For example, CCN, a Nottingham-based direct mail database company keeps details of more than 43 million people, 18 million households, 30 million items of financial information and over 2.5 million personal profiles.[2] Much of this information has been directly taken from government census material, electoral registers and other public sources, but it has been "commodified" in the process.

Allied to the rise in computing power, there is an increased gathering of all kinds of other commercially driven information – on people's buying habits, their attitudes and so on, as is evident in the example given immediately above. There is now a mixed economy for information provision. The public library competes with trade organizations, professional groups, academic centres, business information providers, campaigning and voluntary groups, the Citizens' Advice Bureaux, the Chamber of Commerce and the new DTI-led One Stop shops.

As these other sources of information emerge, the public library is often side-lined. The government policy to establish One Stop shops, for example, largely bypassed the public library service and did not tap into its resources There is a danger that libraries will be left with a mass of broad-based, generalized and unfocused information, while strategic information is withheld and only available for those with the ability to pay.

Commercial imperatives and technological possibilities mean that the individual is usually the target for the new computer-based information industries. Economic logic dictates that it is ultimately more profitable to sell the same product many times over to individual consumers, rather than to a more limited set of public institutions. As Christ Batt has noted, "In the next few years the most important influence on public library use may be the availability of mass market information systems."[3] This is likely to mean that an increasing number of people will have access to new information sources on-line at home or in the office. These developments threaten to bypass information providers that act as intermediaries, such as counter-services (travel agents, banks or building societies) as well as specialist businesses and public libraries. A recent newspaper cartoon showed two elderly people standing in a high street full of boarded-up shops, with one of them reminiscing wistfully, "I remember when this all used to be banks."

Public librarians, if they are to address these questions, need to find mechanisms by which certain classes of users can be protected from the full commercial costs of privatized information. This is not simply a question of protecting public access to information. It is more complex. New kinds of information or products have been created and real costs are involved in the packaging and manipulating of raw data. The "privatization" of information is not a case of turning otherwise public information into paid-for services. It is also about the investment in and creation of new products. How are citizens' rights to information to be determined in a mixed economy in which information is itself a commodity?

Knowledge and power

Since the early 1970s, economists and others have argued that information helps create added value – that the transformation of information into knowledge is equivalent to the transformation of financial and material resources. From this perspective, having access to information, and more importantly the skills to turn this information into knowledge, is the late-twentieth-century equivalent of owning major supplies of coal, iron ore or gold. David Lyon has written that: "The technology-led capacity to supply huge amounts of information in digital form has coincided with the discovery that such information often has a high market value. In other words, data can command a high price as a commodity."[4] Lyon also notes that rather than widening the range of information available to all, the commercial imperative puts a premium on scarcity, secrecy and control: "Now, much of this information, such as that sought for industrial, professional and commercial uses, has its greatest economic value in scarcity rather than widespread distribution."[5]

Further, the great costs of creating databases, cross-referencing and refining them, involves a large capital outlay that can only be amortized through intense competitive selling. Thus, "because it is relatively expensive to establish large databases but relatively cheap to extend the market for services already created, the tendency is towards centralization and monopoly on an international basis".[6]

The supply of information, then, has a political economy of its own, and one of increasing importance in "post-industrial" societies. This has, and will continue, to affect the nature of employment as well as shape the institutions that provide information. As Charles Handy notes in *The age of unreason*:

> Many more clever people are needed – clever people making clever things, or providing clever services that add value with minimal amounts of material. People and organisations making or doing clever things will spend much of their time handling information – facts, figures, words, pictures, ideas, arguments, meetings, committees, papers and conferences. Information and economics are beginning to blend together to create a massive discontinuity in the shape, and skills and purposes of many of our organisations. Clever organisations do not work the way organisations used to work.[7]

The nature of information

Yet information is not an undifferentiated whole. It can be qualitatively divided into levels of value. Information is part of a chain that we use to derive wisdom from the data we find in the world around us. Raw *data* have been defined as "the noise in an informational system". In urban situations, people spend most of their time screening out unwanted data, from the sound of a distant car alarm to the background hum of traffic and machinery.

Data become *information* when they appear potentially relevant to a current situation, and when they become interpretable. In the process of interpreting the information people convert data into *knowledge*. When knowledge becomes generalizable it becomes absorbed as *insight*, which people then carry forward into new situations. If this process enables them to make successful or effective decisions in new and different environments they may be said to have achieved *wisdom*.

This process does not take place separately for each individual. Rather, other people's claimed insights and wisdom are given to us regularly as information that we in turn interpret, and then accept, reject or mutate. The process depends on two complementary aspects. First, we need to have access to data, and in particular to interpretable data in the form of information. Secondly, we need to know how to interpret this information, or be helped to interpret it, before we can absorb it as knowledge we can act upon.

Information, then, is a tool. Increasingly it is an important and a necessary tool to function effectively in society. Access to information, and guidance in the use of information, has always been the core task of the public library. It has never been a more important task than today.

Information and aesthetics

A further complication to this new world of hi-tech information delivery is that the technology is no longer a neutral carrier of inviolable cultural artefacts, but is becoming part of the artefact itself. A book, when handed over the counter as a printed object, portable, with pages sewn in an agreed order and so on, is quite different from the same text downloaded and amenable to reordering, addition and reproduction. When seen at a cinema, the film *Raging bull* is a different cultural object and experience than when viewed on video, fast-forwarded, frozen, replayed and discussed simultaneously by a group of viewers sitting in somebody's front room. The distinctiveness of the cultural form may be being lost in the interactive nature of modern cultural production.

In this scenario, questions of aesthetics appear to become redundant. A text or a film simply become so many bytes or pixels sent down a line and reassembled anew by the individual viewer who creates his or her own unique "reading". In contemporary literary theory, as well as in many versions of post-modernist aesthetics, the role of the cultural producer has moved from the writer to the reader, from the original recording artist to the DJ, sound engineer or mixer. It is no longer the producer who creates aesthetic meanings, but the consumer. It is in this sense that some commentators now talk of everything that the library lends or hires – books, CDs, videos – as all being simply "information". They are anticipating of course; for, mostly, people still want to retain a generic distinction between fiction, documentary and reference within the books they read and use. But a newer world beckons in which more and more of the cultural materials we may wish to read, watch or use will be interactive, or amenable to our own editing or reassembly.

Questions of copyright

All these developments bring into play with greater urgency questions of copyright. Since the means of reproduction – photocopying, home-taping, off-air video taping – have become so widespread and cheap to use, questions on intellectual copyright have become more pressing. Librarians were first alerted to this by the debate as to whether they should lend out records and tapes that could simply be copied at home for free. The music industry has been much more ambivalent about the principle of "free" public library provision of cultural products than the publishing industry. The "blank tape levy" to cover the estimated losses caused to the industry by home-taping has not to date found political favour, and remains unadopted. Yet the issue will not go away.

But the advent of photocopiers in libraries has produced new problems, with the opportunity for library users to photocopy favourite poems, recipes, essays, exam papers, statistics at a much smaller expense than buying the original books. Hence the formal list of proscriptions now to be found next to many library photocopiers informing the user of what can and cannot be legally copied. Commercial photocopy shops are today as alert to these issues, often refusing to photocopy photographs or illustrations from books, and only copying what is proven self-originated text or imagery. Schools have had to buy licences to allow them to record off-air radio and television programmes. Forms of monitoring, policing and collecting fees on behalf of intellectual property rights – such as the Public Lending Right – are likely to grow more sophisticated, particularly as more and more material will be transferred electronically. Scrambling and unscrambling devices, coding and decoding processes, access only by credit card systems will become the norm. Copyright is now such a significant element in international trade that it accounts for 2.5–3% of Britain's GDP.[8]

In Britain and the USA, the rights of reproduction rest with the copyright owners rather than directly with the cultural producers. Hence a comment made by the head of a major American publisher and quoted in the American Journal *Liberal Education*, "We are not a publisher. We are now a creator of copyrights for their exploitation in any medium or distribution system."[9]

The franchised production of goods associated with a major film, for example, are now a central part of the copyright equation associated with major investment in cultural products.

The new means of information delivery

The last decade has seen the introduction of wholly new methods of delivering information. These are all, in one way or another, based on the growing power of personal computers and their lowering price. (In 1983, a 48K Sinclair Spectrum cost £145. Today, a 2-megabyte Apple Macintosh with a 40-megabyte hard disk can be bought for £399. The Macintosh is approximately 50 times more powerful than the Spectrum was.)

The growth of computers capable of manipulating large amounts of information almost instantaneously has a number of important consequences for all information industries. Some everyday information is already publicly available in a computerized form. Both BT's national phone directory and Network SouthEast's timetable can be purchased on floppy disk. Moreover, they can actually be used in ways that are simply not possible with the written directories and timetables: for example, one can search the phone directory by postcode, street name or first name.

The ways in which computers are being used are increasing and, more importantly perhaps, are converging:

- At a recent conference at Bath University, Dr William Arms, a British librarian working in the Carnegie Mellon University in Philadelphia, gave a keynote speech in which he suggested that the cost of storing and retrieving information digitally is on the verge of becoming cheaper and easier than storing it on paper. He said that the university already subscribes to 20 journals that are received only electronically. They are read on screen. People wishing to make "hard copies" do so themselves.
- The "bandwidth" of the cable used for cable television is such that it can carry far more signals than there are television stations. It is capable of carrying many additional channels of digital information: games, entertainment, arts. Nynex, Cablevision and other operators have already begun offering a telephone service that hooks to Mercury for long-distance calls. In 1994 they were getting 20,000 subscribers a month.
- At the beginning of 1992, Philips introduced CD-I. This is one of a number of moves to amalgamate computers, televisions and other electronic consumer goods into a single multimedia device. CD-I players will play audio compact disks; CD-ROMs containing computer data ranging from games to the Guinness Disk of Records to databases and maps; photographs and snapshots processed using Kodak's new photo-CD mechanism (which became available in the high streets in summer 1993). In October 1993, CD-Is were upgraded to enable them to play full-length movies stored on CD-ROMs. The next generation of machines are expected to be able to record as well as play.
- In America in 1994, Project Xanadu began public operation. This project was begun in 1964 by Ted Nelson. It has been described in a number of publications including *Computer Lib*. Its aim is to provide a global publishing and distribution network entirely on screen, with automated royalty payments. It will enable infinite cross-referencing and indexing. It will, as far as Ted Nelson is concerned, replace paper. In so far as it had $50 million spent on it between 1990 and 1995 it cannot be dismissed out of hand.
- Both Sega and Nintendo have plans for the cable or satellite delivery of games and other services. Sega are currently running a pilot Sega TV channel in the USA, with a full channel expected to launch

in 1995. Nintendo are studying the possibility of launching their own satellite network. The aim of these channels is threefold. First, they will enable purchasers to "download" new games, using their games machine and a credit card. Secondly, they will enable people to play games against people in other cities, or other countries. Thirdly, they will enable the introduction of new kinds of entertainment, including (so Nintendo claim) non-fiction information and education.

– The planned introduction of High Definition TV before the year 2000 will go a considerable way to answer arguments about the lack of definition of, and eyestrain caused by, current television screens.

Not all of the developments described above will happen as planned. Some may not happen at all. However, we can be certain that before the end of the twentieth century there will have been significant changes in the ways in which information is published, distributed and used.

It is highly probable that by the early twenty-first century the information landscape will have changed beyond recognition. The library service will need to continue to adapt in order to survive in this new landscape. Not only is there likely to be a major change in the ways in which information is delivered, but this is in turn likely to lead to new ways in which information is perceived and used.

The library of the ether

A sense of the emerging challenges for librarians can be indicated by looking closely at some of the electronic networks such as Internet, which in principle offers extensive opportunities for libraries and librarians by merely adjusting what they already do well to the newer technological environments.

Internet is a network of computer networks. It grew out of a US government-funded experiment, originally developed within the defence industry, to make information freely available and to monitor the effects. The core infrastructure is subsidized by various US government and public agencies. Internet is a completely decentralized and completely global set of interlinked computers. Its primary benefit is that any information stored in any computer in the network can be accessed from any other computer anywhere in the world. Participants include

Table 12.2   On the Internet.

1981 participating institutions/databases	213
1989	80,000
January 1991	313,000
January 1992	376,000
January 1993	727,000

At the beginning of 1995 there are an estimated 10,000,000.

both academic and non-academic libraries, universities, public agencies and financial information providers, and an increasing number of individuals.

To give a sense of the increase in scale of immediately available information resources we only need to look at the growth of information providers attached to the Internet (see Table 12.2).

Beyond these core information providers, referred to as nodes, there are several million users/subscribers. Importantly, Internet also provides the global facility for nodes/subscribers to communicate with each other. This communication can range from the simple posting and receiving of messages through to the electronic publishing of magazines and books (which can be printed out if necessary) to more interactive projects in real time.

The information on Internet stretches from almost all doctoral theses (in the USA), books in electronic formats, government reports and legislation to weather forecasts, financial information and even general information on booking holidays. Many US public libraries have publicly available Internet links. Here the skills of librarians as guides and filterers is of paramount importance.

For example, librarians in Texas helped conduct a series of geography projects in schools linked to parallel projects in Tokyo schools. The National Public Telecomputing Network organized a schools Olympics in track and field events with 52,000 participants in nine countries co-ordinated by Cleveland Free Net and E-mail. At the same time, in these different locations, competitions occurred with overall winners being established.

Significantly, the network has no overall controller. It is merely co-ordinated by a committee, a source of worry to both the CIA and FBI, who feel this "democratic network" has gone out of control. Internet has no physical centre that can be closed down in a time of crisis and it represents an invaluable public space for its users beyond government control. It can be used in the same way that faxes were used by Chinese dissidents in the Tianamen Square uprising, or mobile phones have recently been used in Britain to co-ordinate anti-road campaigns and demonstrations.

Non-linear information

The post-mechanical world involves the replacement of certain mechanical production and distribution mechanisms with electronic systems of apparent equivalence. This equivalence is somewhat illusory, however, for the electronic systems with which we are becoming familiar have radically different potentials from the mechanical systems they are replacing. These differences will be crucial for artists, entertainers and all those involved in the cultural and information industries.

Computer-based electronic systems are effectively new media, which contain the old mechanical media they have apparently replaced. Marshall McLuhan has noted that "the 'content' of any medium is always another medium. The content of writing is speech, just as the written word is the content of the telegraph." He argues that "it is the medium that shapes and controls the scale and form of human association and action". As new media of expression, the post-mechanical means of production have different possibilities, and raise different expectations among both producers and consumers.[10]

Mechanical systems are inherently linear, and the cultural products of these systems carry that linearity with them. A book consists of a series of pages to be read one after another, and the great majority of writers write their books to be read in this way. The reader begins at page one and reads the ordered pages until the last page has been reached. The book has then been finished. To begin a work of fiction again at the beginning would be to read the same story without the surprises but with an ability to savour the authorial techniques and details missed on the first reading.

It has always been possible to stretch or twist linear forms to try to emulate non-linear forms. Laurence Stern attempted just such a thing in the book *Tristam Shandy* (1759–67). More recently the English novelist B. S. Johnson wrote a book that was designed to be read in any order.

The unfortunates was published in a box in the late 1960s, and contained 27 sections. One is marked as the beginning, and one is marked as the end. The reader is invited to shuffle the other 25 sections into a random order before reading the book.

Electronic, post-mechanical systems, however, are *inherently* non-linear, and the cultural products of these systems will carry that non-linearity with them. In a Hypertext "stack" there is no one order in which the stack has to be read, and users looking at one card cannot necessarily know what the next card is, nor can they necessarily retrace their steps nor do they need to be able to find out how many cards there are in the stack. If *The unfortunates* had been produced as a stack, the reader would have seen the trick but not heard the explanation of how it was done.

Indeed, if Johnson were alive to produce such a stack he would undoubtedly realize that the idea behind the work could be extended infinitely further than the format of a book would ever allow. There could be hundreds of separate sections, and the ways in which they were linked could be as complex as the author required. It would be possible, for example, to arrange that the order in which the work was read determined whether or not several characters appeared at all and what the outcome was. In other words, it would be possible to have a dozen different final sections, and use the order in which the work was perused to determine which one was shown each time.

In their non-linearity, hypermedia stacks offer authors the chance to complete the leap that Johnson tried to make – the move away from creating fixed, unchanging single fictions to setting in motion pluralistic, many-dimensional fiction worlds that the user can explore rather than read.

These fictions will be read on screen rather than on paper. This will bring advantages and disadvantages. The disadvantages are that reading from the screen will impose certain attitudes on the readers, as well as requiring them to be near a computer. It will also impose certain stylistic limitations on authors, who may feel the need to write in screen-sized chapters or chunks. It is worth remembering here that authors have never been free of stylistic limitations imposed by the media of production and distribution. The shape and size of Dickens's novels was, for example, determined to a great extent by their publication in serial form in magazines. The length of Scott Fitzgerald's *Pat Hobby* stories was determined by the editorial requirements of *Esquire*.

The advantages are the additional scope offered to enrich imaginative work. There need be no more fear of footnotes cluttering up a work, since they can be hidden until they are needed. This facility can be greatly expanded. In another of his books, *Christy Muldoon's double entry*, Johnson offers asides about the characters as the story unfolds. It would be possible to extend this by offering layered footnotes about each character. Clicking on the name of any character might open up a skeletal biography of that character prior to the start of the novel. Clicking on aspects of that biography might lead on to further details, or complete other stories. In a work where the focus is on a milieu and how characters live within it, this kind of device might be used to show how they interact with others, and how complex are the relationships between them.

If hypermedia allow artists to tell stories in a complex and non-linear way, through which readers can thread their own idiosyncratic way, then similar non-linear possibilities open up with regard to the organization of actual information. Instead of footnotes explaining the source of a quotation, the reader could flip to the actual page of the original book from which the quotation is drawn, offering the possibility of checking that it has not been torn from its context. If the name of a politician is mentioned, it should be possible to click on the name and read a short biography. Clicking on any of the items in the biography would bring up an expanded account.

Needs and demands

One of the major issues raised by current technological developments is the ways in which information is actually used, and the kinds of information that people really need. Too often in the past, the development of information systems has been seen as a specialist "technical" job, rather than as a cultural activity of general importance.

Centralized databases and "on-line" services work from a specific set of presuppositions. They assume that the available data will be managed centrally; that the data will be made available according to predefined criteria; that users will access data according to prescribed rules. They allow the information to be updated frequently – every few minutes if necessary.

These services have ongoing costs in terms of inputting information, monitoring the system, maintaining the equipment and dealing with user enquiries. Usually access to information in this way is charged per minute, encouraging precisely targeted enquiries and penalizing browsing. An example of this kind of system being used successfully is the subset of Prestel used by travel agents to monitor flight and accommodation availability on screen.

The decentralized distribution of information through CD-ROMs has different structural implications. It does not require constant administration or overseeing. It does not penalize browsing, since users pay once for the disk that they are then free to use as, when and how they please. On the other hand, the information on the disk cannot be updated, except through the replacement of the disk with a new edition.

Unlimited bandwidth

If systems such as those described above come to fruition in the ways currently envisaged, then there will be a major shift in terms of the ways in which information is published and distributed nationally and internationally. Since the introduction of printed books in the fourteenth century, the notion of publication has always implied a filtering process based upon scarcity. Printing presses cost money; paper costs money; transporting and storing books costs money. There have, therefore, always been more people wanting to publish material than were able to; and the status of published author was often keenly sought.

In the current jargon, the book trade has always had a "narrow bandwidth". The advent of electronic publishing, however, raises the prospects of a medium of distribution of almost unlimited bandwidth.

Al Gore's information superhighway project is being talked of in terms of delivering *several thousand* television or information channels to every home in America. Video-on-demand technology is being projected to download a 90-minute movie in 30 seconds. That means that each of the several thousand information channels could deliver 2,880 movies a day, every day of the year; or hundreds of thousands of books, records, databases, etc.

The cost of storing and moving information electronically is already minute compared to the cost of traditional publishing. All that is currently lacking is a suitable set of delivery systems with which people are happy, and with which they feel comfortable. At that point anything that can be published will be published, and the notion of publication as a filtering process will vanish.

Librarians and information

At first glance, it might appear that the scenario sketched above will make the public library as old-fashioned as the horse-drawn buggy. It might be expected that everybody will sit at home directly downloading or uploading whatever they desire. This, however, is extremely unlikely, for two reasons.

First, solitary activity is likely to be eclipsed by shared activity, if only because most people tend to reject solitary pursuits in favour of shared activity. The idea that children will lock themselves away in rooms on their own for hours to play computer games says more about the current state of technological development in this field than it does about children's desires to be hermits. As soon as the technology permitted it, two-player games were introduced, and became unsurprisingly popular. At this point computers or games consoles retreat to being tools for play, in the way that toy soldiers, dolls and yo-yos have been tools for play for previous generations. In a similar way, computers will retreat to being information tools as the technophobia of previous generations disappears.

Secondly, as the information networks grow richer, people will need more help and guidance in finding what they need or want. People will increasingly need information about where to find the right information. As Batt notes, "The occasional user will be lost and will need the help of 'warm bodies' (the current jargon for you and me)".[11] This has always been an important part of the librarian's role, and has been an acknowledged part of the public library service since Dewey introduced the decimal index cataloguing system.

Knowledge navigators

In an information age based on the notion of unlimited oceans of information through which readers or users can chart their own course, there will be a need for "knowledge navigators" – people who have mapped the flow of information and know where the currents lead. This role has always been at the core of librarianship, and the need for it will grow rather than shrink.

The Dewey decimal index system was a bold attempt to produce a system of information that catalogued and made comprehensible a large amount of information that might otherwise have appeared so large as to be unapproachable. There is a growing need for a similar system to map the growing worldwide information network, and to provide access to it for ordinary people. In order to provide this access, libraries may change and mutate beyond recognition, but at their core there will still need to be a group of "knowledge navigators" – librarians.

CHAPTER 13

Other worlds:
libraries, fiction and popular reading

Libraries play an important part in the cultural enrichment of people's lives, and although this takes many forms, in our study we chose to concentrate on the arguments about the importance of popular fiction, as this remains one of the most contested areas of library provision, particularly in regard to whether this is a genuine "public good", and thus eligible to be funded out of general taxation.

The popularity of popular fiction

In 1990–1, 561 million books were issued by public libraries in the United Kingdom. Of these, by far the biggest single category of loans, 59%, were for adult fiction. And of these novels, the majority were what is currently termed "genre fiction": crime novels, romance, family sagas, adventure novels. In 1992, the five most borrowed authors were Catherine Cookson, Agatha Christie, Danielle Steel, Dick Francis and Ruth Rendell. According to John Sumsion, now at the Library and Information Statistics Unit at Loughborough University of Technology, none of the top 100 novels borrowed, according to Public Lending Right statistics, were "literary novels". The overwhelming popularity of genre fiction is an established fact, yet it continues to cause embarrassment among some librarians, and an ambivalence and equivocation when it comes to formulating policy statements.

Given the deep unease that the popularity of genre fiction causes the library profession, it is quite extraordinary that decisions as to whether to promote, divert attention from, or reduce genre fiction stocks are seemingly made with no evidence at all as to what readers derive from these books. The reader's point of view is always missing from these debates. Why?

In fact, the librarian's ambivalence about genre fiction originates in an ambivalence about fiction itself. The historical emphasis on the educational role of the public library has meant a preoccupation with instrumental knowledge; the role of the library in providing fiction, particularly fiction of an "entertaining" or "recreational" nature, remains contested even to this day. Pat Coleman, until recently Director of Library Services in Birmingham, for example, recalled her early days as a librarian in Manchester at the beginning of the 1970s:

> We used to have the fiction and the non-fiction shelved in alter-
> nate rows. This was in the hope that someone who came in for
> fiction might one day actually find themselves in the non-fiction
> and take a non-fiction book out by mistake and suddenly find
> that their life had been changed as a result of this experience. We
> also used to count the loans of non-fiction separately from fic-
> tion and we used to look at the end of every day to see how much
> the non-fiction loan total had gone up. We gave people more
> tickets for borrowing non-fiction than fiction . . . The main
> emphasis of our book selection was on non-fiction and that was
> true of the collection development policy generally.[1]

This was the 1970s, remember, not the 1870s. At the 1992 Scottish Library Conference in Aberdeen, to mark the centenary of Aberdeen Public Library, the historian Raphael Samuel tactfully reminded the audience that for some years following publication, the novels of Lewis Grassic Gibbon – Aberdeen's most famous literary son – were not available in the local public library. For many librarians, fiction is still the ghost at the banquet, the irreverent intruder into a more dignified gathering.

The paperback revolution

The traditional ambiguity about fiction, which has informed much library provision, was compounded in the 1950s by the arrival of the paperback novel. In many ways, libraries are still adjusting to the paperback revolution, an event that happened over fifty years ago. As Hans Schmoller has written: "It is not in dispute, however, that the publication by Allen Lane of the first ten Penguins in 1935 was the event to which virtually all paperback developments in the western world during the past forty years can be traced."[2]

It should be remembered that paperbacks were launched with great opposition from the publishing and bookselling worlds. The *Bookseller* magazine at the time reminded its readers that "many booksellers, it is known, do not regard very cheap reprints with favour".[3] If the bookselling world did not like paperbacks, librarians were no more happy with them either. It took nearly fifty years from the advent of Penguins for librarians to welcome paperbacks on to their own bookshelves. Largely, this was because of the durability of the soft-covered books, but it was also to do with content, as John Sutherland's important study *Fiction and the fiction industry*, has shown:

> The paperback revolution of the late 1950s and 1960s gained much of its energy from fiction that the public library could be expected to disapprove of: *Woman of Rome, The Ginger Man, Lolita, Lady Chatterley's Lover, The Naked and the Dead, Catch 22, Candy.* Anyone who wanted to keep up with the moving frontiers of permissive fiction was forced out of the libraries; paperbacks often had the glamour, as it were, of an informal *Index Librorum Prohibitorum.*[4]

Even today it sometimes appears that librarians are happier with the back catalogue of fiction than with the literary avant-garde, the sensationally new, or contemporary genres. In the course of this study, several librarians pointed out – with a sense of justified grievance – that librarians are rarely represented on the panels of the great literary prizes, on the panels of poetry competitions or even in sufficient numbers on Arts Council or Regional Arts Board literary advisory panels. Yet librarians are among the foremost mediators of fiction within the literary world.

Romance on the rates?

Adult fiction is equally contentious for the librarian because there are, *prima facie*, very few arguments as to why the public lending of such books for free should be regarded as a quintessential "public good", and therefore eligible for subsidy out of taxes. It is not difficult to muster arguments as to the educational and/or civic benefits of lending instructional material, history, sociology and so on, as well as providing reference materials for free, but the case for fiction is more difficult. Librarians have not helped by withdrawing from many of the important debates about fiction, to the point where it is possible for an informed critic to assert that "as a specialism, the art of selecting novels for adults is virtually dead in public libraries, although it flourishes in the field of children's fiction".[5]

Yet there *are* important arguments for continuing to provide fiction for free as a core library service. These can be summarized as follows:

- For many library users, borrowing a novel is just part of a wider usage pattern – the "mixed bag" – that includes taking out non-fiction and using the library's reference services. Charging for fiction could create a form of "cultural apartheid" within the library, building barriers and reducing choice.
- It is fiction-lending that provides the public library with its wide audience catchment, and thus provides a critical mass of users that gives the library its comfortable social atmosphere.
- The assumption that the "market place" could compensate for the withdrawal of fiction stocks from public libraries, or the charging of a "commercial" lending fee, is not convincing. The evidence of our study is that for many people, particularly those living in areas of multiple deprivation, high levels of fiction borrowing and reading fulfil a social need that would be much more costly to provide in terms of conventional "welfare" support.
- Fiction does not simply "entertain" or "amuse", but fulfils many other functions for the reader, some of which are strongly educational, developmental, therapeutic, life-enhancing and a part of a shared intellectual citizenship.
- Fiction is not an undifferentiated category. There are all kinds of novels – science fiction, crime, historical, utopian, war, romantic, instructional, philosophical – many of which explore areas of human experience in ways that "factual" books cannot, and which

133

have multiple meanings and multiple effects. Any attempt to divide fiction into "serious" and "escapist" for the purposes of levying charges or to inform stock-holding policy would be intellectually impossible.

The active role of the reader

To the outsider it seems that the world of librarianship has been sheltered from, or chosen to exclude itself from, many of the most important developments in post-war literary criticism. These have shifted attention away from the intentions of the writer as the primary object of scrutiny when discussing the literary value of particular books, to the active and creative role played by the reader. The "death of the author" and the discovery of the creative reader, however, is not fully acknowledged in library debates. Yet without knowing much more fully what the millions of readers of popular fiction are deriving from their avid reading patterns, formulating policy about fiction stocks is almost impossible.

In the course of the study, Comedia commissioned the writer Rebecca O'Rourke to summarize current research on popular fiction readership, and to map out some ways of characterizing the important part that genre fiction plays in people's lives. She also interviewed library users in Cleveland about their reading. The results were published as Working Paper 7, but her views in summary were:

– The popularity of much genre fiction derives from the familiarity of its working class-settings, the sense of stoicism in adversity, and of generational change and flux of family fortunes (e.g. Lena Kennedy, Catherine Cookson).

"It takes me back to my young days. I see a lot of myself in these books."
"The history's what I read them for. You realise how lucky we've been."
"It's my life really, really down to earth, Northern life."
"That was my generation, and I was in the Navy too."
(Readers, Cleveland libraries)

– Reading (of whatever kind) is a way of demarcating a form of personal space within the home, a way of cutting off from demands on time and energy from other family members.

"I like them because they're not too difficult. With work to do and a child, I can pick them up and put them down."

"It's an easy read, a way to unwind from the kids in the bath or in a spare five minutes."

"It's a form of relaxation for me. I have a very demanding job."

(Women, Cleveland libraries)

– "Escapist" fiction does precisely that: it allows people to enter into worlds of their own imagination, to detach themselves from daily privations and disappointments.

"Romance is definitely my favourite. Sometimes I think it's all just the same old story and then I might not read anything for a while but I always come back to romance. It's something I haven't got – money, travel, all that. I know it isn't real, but you don't think of that as you're reading it."

"I prefer it to TV because I can use my own imagination. It's good for you and it's entertaining. I'll read anything as long as it's not filth."

(Women, Cleveland libraries)

– Popular fiction can provide an insight into cultures and experiences that might otherwise never be directly encountered.

"I like books set in different countries or cultures so you can learn something as well as enjoy the story."

"I like – you know, the Jewish one – Maisie Mosco. It just fascinates me, I don't know why. I love reading about all their ways. How else would I learn about Jewish people?"

(Women, Cleveland libraries)

– It is often only part of a mixed collection of books borrowed; genre fiction readers are also borrowers of other library books, and users of other library services.

"I'll read anything, but I like romance especially. I know people disapprove but it's very readable."

(Woman, Cleveland libraries)[6]

Rebecca O'Rourke's research was undertaken in Cleveland, and coincided with the Cleveland case study, which also highlighted the important role that genre fiction played in borrowings from small neighbourhood libraries, often in areas of high social and economic disadvantage. Cultural enrichment takes many forms, and it was revealed in

the study that the provision of fiction has many meanings and influences, far wider than was originally understood. We would argue that
the emotional and psychological benefits of genre fiction reading –
essentially the age-old pleasures of story-telling, myth, fairy tale and
fable – are very much at the centre of the benefits that the public library
offers to people, particularly to those who have neither financial nor
physical access to a constant supply of bookshop fiction, especially
when for many people we met and talked to, a week's Income Support
benefit would hardly cover the cost of a single hardback.

PART 5

Tomorrow's world

CHAPTER 14

Past, present and future

So while an older world is dying, the new world still struggles to be born. Modern society is still, in many ways, an incomplete project, irrespective of talk about postmodern culture. For quite early in the study we realized – an impression more than confirmed by some of the press reactions to the consultative report – that public libraries, like many other public and commercial institutions, carry with them a heavy baggage of popular perceptions, misperceptions and mythologies, which it is still generally difficult for them to escape or dispel. British society is still heavy with what are perceived to be ageing and unmodernized institutions – the public schools, British Rail, the DHSS, the House of Lords, among many examples that could be given – which have all been mythologized for good or bad within the British psyche. So too has the public library. One of the more self-punishing myths of contemporary British intellectual culture is that of "the decline of the public library", a powerful nostrum that is five parts nostalgia, four parts metropolitan myopia, and only one part fact. The strength of a received and powerfully influential set of associations and beliefs about the public library came across very strongly in some of the press comments on the *Borrowed time?* report. It would not be difficult to argue that this mythology is now deeply counter-productive to the library cause, and what is urgently needed is a "repositioning" of the library within contemporary social attitudes, and the urgent need for public librarians to cultivate a "new set of friends". It was always the intention of this book to develop the intellectual framework for this new culture and the intellectual rationale for public library provision for the future.

The prevalent mythology surrounding the public library, as expressed in many of these reviews and columns, included the following elements:

– *A lost world of silence and furniture polish* Many contemporary columnists writing about public libraries – all men it was interesting to note – consistently evoked a world we have lost. Keith Waterhouse writing in the *Daily Mail* remembered "a haven of peace smelling of Mansion polish with not a sound to be heard except the steady thump-thump-thump of rubber stamp on flyleaf".[1] Martyn Harris writing in the *Daily Telegraph* harked back affectionately to "the austere and orderly library with its clacking parquet floors and smell of beeswax polish; the soft-eared cardboard library pass that was the first badge of adulthood".[2] In the *Observer*, Jonathan Keates recalled that "The public library in Graham Road, Great Malvern, the decayed spa town where we lived, became a shrine, enough to set the heart racing as we unlatched the white gate at the top of its high-hedged garden, raced down the path past the war memorial and burst through swing-doors into the crepuscular gloom."[3] A leader in *The Times* warned that "the life of quiet contemplation libraries have long stood for seems to be under threat".[4]

– *A terrifying seedbed of political correctness* Yet today, such writers saw only change and decay wherever they looked, with Waterhouse stereotyping at every turn:

Nowadays the local library is likely to be a cultural slum, festooned with realms of print-out paper and leaflets offering information on the nearest gypsy encampment, its tattered books being gradually edged out by videos and compact discs, its be-jeaned, earring sporting assistants treating their "customers" to the self-righteous evangelical smile of the Politically Correct and whining for more "resources".

Martyn Harris was no less happy, characterizing the report's description of the modern library as being "the familiar picture of the library as a right-on crèche for latchkey children, the 'unwaged', single mothers and what the report calls 'an entry point to the wider culture for many of Britain's ethnic minority communities'". Later on, Harris described the library where he lives: "Hornsey, of course, is beige tin and plastic with acres of tattered notices advertising Tai Chi, Feminist Massage, and *Practical Magic*."

– *Good old-fashioned books* All of the commentators regretted the move that many libraries have made into stocking records, CDs, tapes, videos and other kinds of materials. In the *Observer*, Donald Fisher regretted that:

> Those who love books, however, may have been unthinking accomplices in this devaluation of the printed word . . . Libraries have changed out of all recognition in the past 20 years . . . Libraries are "learning centres". You can borrow records, tapes, videos. Some even have muzak, like lifts in irritating hotels. You can photocopy documents, admire exhibitions of work from the local art society, gaze at flower arrangements, send and receive faxes, buy unwanted copies of quite valuable books for a few pence and thrill to read the broadsheet of the area's Training and Enterprise Council. Diversification has gone too far.[5]

Roy Hattersley writing in the *Guardian* concurred, threatening a withdrawal of love from the library profession as if from a wayward child: "However, the high esteem in which I hold them is entirely the result of their close proximity to books. Further loosening of that relationship will diminish rather than increase my affection."[6] Keith Waterhouse was less measured, describing his local library with "its tattered books slowly being edged out by videos and compact discs". Martyn Harris issued a call to arms: "Throw out the video libraries, the 'feminist book' sections, the fragile and expensive children's books, and the money-pit microcomputers."

Some observations are in order. First, as has been noted, almost all of the people who have written about libraries in the press – usually columnists or editorial writers – were men, generally older men. Invariably they recalled, and then compared, the library of their childhood (often in a provincial town or city in the 1940s or 1950s) with the library in London where they lived today (much more likely to be in a multi-racial area and therefore quite different in social composition from the one of their childhood). They were not comparing like with like but believed they were. What they were often expressing was their own sense of dislocation and disillusionment, or, as Wordsworth might have expressed it, "the shades of the prison house closing in". They had lost their youth, and they were lashing out. What they wanted was, in fact, a library for older men: they didn't want children's picture books, feminist books, notices about gypsies or massage, information for the unemployed or single mothers, videos or compact disks, computers, or young male library assistants with earrings. What they were expressing was hatred of the modern world, but they were projecting this on to the changes that have happened in the natural development of the modern public library in accommodating to new forms of communication and new social needs.

One might also ask, how wonderful really was this library of their youth, which brought out such an excess of purple in their columnist's prose? According to someone who was there at the time, a writer whose judgement they would doubtless trust, it is worth recalling Philip Larkin's version of that halcyon library of the 1940s: "I spend most of my time handing out tripey novels to morons."[7] All this would be humorous if it were not still so pervasive and influential. The debate about public libraries, we realized, is still in many ways dominated and engineered by people who dislike most forms of social change, and it therefore becomes imperative that the public library movement urgently promotes a more dynamic and modern image of itself, cultivates opinion-formers among the younger generation, and proclaims its cultural modernism with pride rather than defensiveness and evasion.

Yet the move towards modernization is fraught with difficulty. What kinds of social trends will shape tomorrow's world? Are public cultural institutions and facilities such as libraries, museums and parks struggling against a current that is rushing towards the commodification and marketization of every aspect of life? These institutions are not wholly instrumental or over-determined; rather they create places and time for incidental activity, as we have tried to demonstrate in Chapter 9. Their ethos is drawn from an older sense of respect for a citizen's right simply to be there without having to pay or justify one's presence. How will institutions such as these fare in the future?

For *public libraries are institutions whose functions appear to be fundamentally challenged by continuing technological and social changes.* Their purpose in the modern world has been questioned, for example by the Adam Smith Institute, and the scale of public funding devoted to the service may in future be queried. All public expenditure is likely to be under closer scrutiny. Identifying the future rationale and cultural position of the public library, therefore, is essential.

142

The non-predictable future

How should public libraries plan for the future? In the past, many organizations made plans based on the assumption that the current trends would develop in a linear manner. This led to what is now seen as a somewhat cumbersome model, with plans being laid in the expectation that the operating environment would produce predictable outcomes, in a world whose self-image was reinforced by set patterns of thinking – ideologies, Cold War blocs – and a sense of historical permanence and continuity.

Yet the world now seems to be changing in decisive but unpredictable ways. We are less sure of ourselves and of the institutions that formed part of our known environment. How is this new phase characterized? And how can the public library fit in? We can already feel the period we are entering in outline: the sense of a deeper structural change with a greater degree of impermanence, a greater degree of flexibility in work styles, flatter, less hierarchically based organizations, and much greater mobility. All this changes what we mean by communities. Communities are likely to be formed around confluences of interest rather than determined by geographic locations. At the same time there is a renewed search for more enduring values that buck the seemingly endless and hectic pace of change. As always, any trend embodies its counter-trend – but will it be too late to save the very best of the past in terms of public service and public institutions, which may by then have disappeared for ever?

Flexible, anticipatory and experimental

What does this kind of scenario mean in terms of planning for the library of the future? It means a recognition that strategy formation needs to be flexible, anticipatory and experimental. Needs will emerge and subtly change. Libraries will need to be more process oriented; they will need to talk to their users more often. In some sense this represents a paradigm shift, and it appears that we may be entering such a period now. The majority of libraries do not appear to be aware of the significance of these changes or to respond accordingly.

Knowing about the future is essential for libraries. Even libraries live in a competitive environment. An assessment of the typology of cultural institutions over time reveals how institutions both rise and fall and how their status and comparative funding can change. Their decline or growth depends on how institutions can make their activities appear relevant to their contemporary world. Few institutions are permanent.

Being seen as relevant is important, because from that funding flows. And the library could be made more relevant again. As the reaction against the trend to be constantly instrumental (effective, efficient) and productive in terms of measurable outcomes grows, and time for the informal, the incidental, for browsing and exploration seems ever more precious, so the role of the library could move centre stage.

But public libraries must get beyond fads and fashion and analyze underlying trends and deeper structural changes. Here we need to recognize the importance of inter-generational shifts, as Ronald Inglehart so aptly describes in his book *Cultural shifts*[8] – a generation brought up on audio-visual culture, computers and increasingly instant information has a different relationship to the book than a 1930s' bibliophile. This does not mean the book will die, but its relative role as a medium of information exchange will alter. And the look of places built for books – libraries – is likely to change also.

The influence and importance of political and strategic choices and positioning are still paramount. Libraries need to be aware of change in all kinds of spheres, as each represents an opportunity to grasp or a threat to avoid. Public libraries need to be aware of cyclical changes such as economic growth patterns; linear changes such as the shift from manufacturing to services or population growth; and non-linear changes, such as changing attitudes to work. These will all affect the role and positioning of public libraries.

The forces of change

Which forces and issues are the real motors of change? We highlight a few.

- *Population change* Population growth and population movement continue apace even in Britain, and while we may not experience the growth of mega-cities evident in the Third World, pressures will persist on our less populated areas, especially market towns. Most cities in the United Kingdom will continue to lose population – although this trend is now slowing down – and some city centres will shift, if the movement towards out of town is not curtailed. What do we do in places where a public library has lost its audience and natural catchment area?

The age structure is shifting towards older people. The baby boomers of the 1950s and 1960s are ageing and as the birth rate declines and is predicted to fall dramatically, there will be more older people. In 1995 the majority of adults (16+) in the United Kingdom will be over 45 and the elderly will increase from 10.5 million in 1994 to 13 million in 2021, causing a fall in the worker: pensioner ratio. This will create a caring crisis, especially for women (who live longer), and doubts about the capacity of the working population to support the rest.

There are greater numbers of self-employed, rising from 1.9 million in 1979 to 3.1 million in 1988. There are more single-person households, from 12% in 1961 to 26% in 1988; fewer larger families, from 15% in 1961 to 7% in 1988; more interest in pressure groups according to the report *British social attitudes 1994*; more individual home ownership, from 43% in 1961 to 65% in 1988, and so on. The public library, sensitive to social and demographic shifts, will have to adapt its services – opening times, support services – accordingly.[9]

– *The nature of employment* The nature of employment is changing with a predicted rockbed of unemployment and under-employment; there is a move to more flexible work patterns, as outlined for example in Charles Handy's classic *The future of work*;[10] there will be a move towards life-long learning. These changes highlight the need for continual retraining and a trend towards tele-commuting and working from home.

There are continuing and substantial inequalities of poverty and wealth. The income of the poorest 10% has grown more slowly than that of those who are better off – 2.6% against 5.4%. There is already talk of the rise of the "two-thirds" society, not just in Britain but in many other developed countries of the world, with a third of the population in permanent unemployment, while the rest do relatively well. There is no policy for full employment on the horizon, although all political parties are now competing to develop one, as

145

the political indifference to unemployment shown in the 1980s is now understood to have been disastrous in social terms. There is a higher level of "acceptable" unemployment now, and there are more long-term unemployed as a proportion of the unemployed population – 25% in 1979 and 40% in 1991. In the past, the public library has focused on those without access to other resources. What are the implications for public libraries of this rockbed of unemployment?[11]

– *Quality of life* Nations, cities, private companies or public entities will battle out their relative positioning less on the basis of "natural" comparative advantage, such as existing resources, location or past reputation, and more according to their ability to "create comparative advantage". This will depend on their capacity to create images or their ability to market themselves in a world increasingly dominated by media imagery. They will base their competitive edge on how they can project themselves as part of an increased "quality of life". As knowledge will be part of that future "quality", public libraries have an initial advantage, in that they clearly are valued and do perform vital services, but they need to let the world know about it.

– *Public sphere versus marketization* The public sphere will be under threat as every facet of life is marketized and swept up by commodification. There is the continual threat that business will vacuum up every aspect of "authenticity" – and turn it into a product. There will be a shift from "the natural fabric of life to a sense of community paid for with a price".[12]

Public libraries flourished in a period when the cost of books was still high in relation to disposable income – that equation has now changed. Commercial forces, through the techniques of direct marketing aided by computing power, are driving products and services towards individual consumers at their home – bypassing intermediaries like libraries and retailers. In this situation, public libraries need to redirect their goals and services to provide opportunities that "at home" cannot provide.

Of course, there will be counter-trends. Yet the trend in the foreseeable future goes against what is loftily called the "public sphere". The idea of the public sphere feels as if it lacks a function; it appears not to be aimed towards a measurable, instrumental target; it feels as if it has no calculable worth. It falls so easily into the idea of the social, the community and a number of other soft concepts – not focused or hard edged. Yet, more often than not when people are interviewed outside the pressures of their job and when barriers are down they admit to a yearning for a sense of community. Again, in the 1990s all of the major political parties in the United Kingdom are competing to represent these "softer" values and re-emphasize their importance.

– *Sustainability* Then there is also the need to absorb the full implications of greenness, the challenge of sustainability where "quality of life" issues highlight concerns beyond economic growth. Sustainability development arguments, popularized most publicly by the Brundlandt Report, might change the nature of our aspirations and how the First World deals with the Second and the Third Worlds. What will be the new indicators of success that go beyond GNP calculations? David Pearce's book *Blueprint: 3 – measuring sustainable development* is a concerted attempt to address these issues.[13] Public libraries, with their culture of borrowing rather than buying, could be exemplars of a new attitude.

– *Globalization* The top 500 companies now control 60% of world production. Will it be the top 250 in ten years, or will there be a focus on networking and strategic alliances? It looks that way at the moment. Every company or institution needs to have the capacity to feel bigger than it actually is. It needs to be networked. And so do public libraries. Global communications are now a reality – yet not everybody will be part of the global village. What are the implications? For public libraries this means confronting global communications, not only for the sake of being international, but also because now being local and responding to local needs means equally being aware of global trends.

Significantly, while economics is globalizing, politics and associated structures are finding it difficult to keep up. A myriad of laws, regulations and counter-regulations is one measure of the current confusion – creating a true information maze. One potential role for the public library lies in assisting guiding us through the skein of directives coming out of the European Union. It has also been argued that the best hope for Britain's public library service at a strategic level lies in its Europeanization, its connections and structural relationships and networks with European programmes and funding regimes, rather than with what could be a continuing policy of national indifference.

– *New identities* Nationalism, regionalism and internationalism are replaying themselves out in Europe in a dangerous game of identities. This is a problem that will not go away in the shorter term. Increased mobility fosters the new nationalism and will create future difficulties for multiculturalism. The public library, as we have seen, is a key entry point for new members of society. It can help smooth paths to understanding and acceptance in the larger society.

The focus on "authenticity" for good and for bad: is this the true response to modernism and its insecurities and rapid change? Identity, locality, nationalism and uniqueness are again put centre stage. Hastened by the collapse of Communism in the East, nationalisms curtailed are, for example, re-emerging with a vengeance. Interestingly, the last stumbling block to the GATT negotiations was a cultural–identity issue, the right for audio-visual products in Europe to be omitted from a free trade treaty. What will the library response be to these pressures?

– *Knowledge is capital* Our society has not yet fully absorbed the implications of this developing shift. It is similar in importance to the shift from the feudal economy based on barter and political patronage to the mercantile economy based on money exchange. Knowledge as the key source of power and wealth focuses our attention sharply on the need to control and have access to information sources in whatever form they be. "Access to information or perish" might be a suitable rendition of a well-worn cliché. Who are the gatekeepers to knowledge? We know that librarians are and could be more so. Access to knowledge is now the strategic resource, especially in countries whose manufacturing base has declined. Knowledge is a resource as once the coalmines were, or the capacity to grow food.

– *Education and training* There is a shift to the Pacific Rim, which is good for Japan, South-East Asia and Australia. Where does that leave poor old Europe? Why is the "Rim" taking over? Some of the reasons canvassed include that it invests more in education, more in information gathering and, it appears, more in strategic thinking. Again, a role for public libraries seems self-evident.

A training crisis will emerge as Britain attempts to compete with the rest of the world, as the economy of the future will require a highly skilled workforce. And as the relative number of school leavers declines, measures will be introduced to retain older workers and women after maternity leave and to encourage those at home to return to work. In 1987, 64% of women of working age were working, compared with 58% in 1981. This may well reach 75% by 1995. And women will account for 90% of net additions to the workforce between 1988 and 1995.[14] The percentage of the UK labour force having occupational qualifications is very low compared with Germany, France, The Netherlands, Italy and Spain, as was shown in Chapter 11.

– *Organizational change* Organizing for chaos and uncertainty. Tom Peters, J. Gleick and Charles Handy, amongst many, have all written that existing organizational structures seem to be inadequate to deal with the range of problems that will be presented to them in the future. There will be a need to reorganize, rethink structures, rethink relationships to work and create less hierarchical structures, and of course a need to build strategic alliances with other institutions and interest groups in both the public and commercial spheres.

We do not know how these conflicts and trends will pan out, but as we have hoped to show in this book, the public library is ideally located to be in the forefront of the structural response to these changes. In spite of changes in the economic and technological structure of our societies, public libraries still embody long-standing principles, such as, for example, free access to a collectively provided public good, whose merits although currently obscured will, we think, return. In the meantime, though, it is important to understand how a renewed public sector might develop, and how public cultural institutions in particular may need to adapt in order to survive. In the next chapter we return again to the defining characteristics of public sector institutions, and the struggles they are currently engaged in, in order to find a new role for themselves in the twenty-first century.

CHAPTER 15

The modern state and
new meanings of the public

Many of the ideas in this chapter owe much to Geoff Mulgan's paper *The public service ethos and public libraries*. The apparently simple idea of a public is in fact beset by contradictions. Perhaps the most basic contradiction in our notion of the public arises from the sociological and political divide that accompanied the birth of the modern state and civil society. This was well described by Daniel Bell, who wrote that the distinctive feature of the modern market economy, in sociological terms, is that "It has been a bourgeois economy. This has meant two things: first that the ends of production are not common but individual; and second, that the motives for the acquisition of goods are not needs but wants."[1] The wants and desires of individuals are thus put centre stage.

However, it was this same bourgeoisie that came to define much of what we now mean by a public space. It did so in its struggle in the eighteenth century to create what Jürgen Habermas has called a "public sphere of discourse". Habermas defined this as "a realm of our social life in which something approaching public opinion can be formed . . . a portion of the public sphere comes into being in every conversation in which private individuals assemble to form a public body".[2] The public libraries, public museums and public art galleries, emerging in the nineteenth century, epitomized this public sphere.

According to Habermas, this world of free and rational discourse was undermined by its own success. As the bourgeoisie grew and capital began to move into the means of communication, the structure of the media changed and with it the nature of public discourse. Advertising became the primary source of revenue for newspapers and magazines.

Ownership became concentrated. Newspapers were increasingly seen as indistinguishable from other business activities, their goals commercial rather than political. Newspapers changed too from being retailers of news to becoming dealers in public opinion and ultimately a medium of consumer culture. Indeed, it is now a complaint of modern societies that it is newspapers that mould government opinion – and in some cases hire and fire ministers – rather than the other way round.

Yet the bourgeoisie remained committed to the principles that had served it well and that seemed threatened by an evolving mass media and the logic of property development. The market had ceased to be guarantor of the public sphere and had, instead, become a threat. This, Habermas argues, was the logic that led to the state being called in as a bulwark against the encroachment of commercialism. Public education and public libraries were mobilized as the bearers of the principles of rational public discourse, of a space insulated from the logic of the market place under the aegis of the state. Later public service radio and television, and in some countries subsidized arts and cinema, would play similar roles. Interestingly, the cause of public libraries and the cause of public service broadcasting in Britain have often been yoked together as representing the very best of the "public service" ideal, culturally eclectic, and embodying the Reithian principles to "inform, educate and entertain".

Public service in culture and communications had two dimensions. One was an ethos of selfless service, rationality and an elevated and rather abstract idea of the public good involving a concern for the national identity and detachment from vested interests. The second was a set of principles about provision: geographical and social universality, and the provision for minorities as well as majorities. Both of these are to be found at the heart of the public library ideal.

What was always missing from these definitions was any sense of public control or direct democratic accountability between public servants and their public. Instead, control rested with managers and specialists, intellectuals, librarians and engineers: the ethos and rules of professions. In the United Kingdom, which pioneered many of these ideas, three kinds of structure took shape: public service libraries and educational institutions run by strong professional groups informed by a clear mission of improvement; a public service broadcasting organization under the control of an independent board; and a public telephone company originally under the Post Office, a pioneer in the new forms of management but one that took many of its organizational forms from the Civil Service and defined its publicness in terms of rules of provision. But this describes something that is public in ethos rather than control.

New arguments in the public interest

Any redefinition of the public is therefore not easily detached from its bearings. The older definitions are clearly much embedded in particular traditions and histories, balances of forces and competing ethical systems.

But the history does at least show the minimum conditions for any coherent account of the public interest argument:

- First, the public interest has simultaneously to articulate a vision of society and explain the nature of the communities within it as well as why these share interests that are not likely to be met by atomized market provision; these may be multiple communities but they must be more than aggregates of individuals if the argument is not to fall back simply on to an "economy of scale" argument about public goods.

- Secondly, it has to generate credible rules of provision: credible in that they do not simply extrapolate from the simple monomedia origins of the libraries in a print culture to the coexistence of multiple media cultures in the future; credible too in that they are politically sustainable, for example by maintaining the political support of dominant social groups or "swing groups", as has been vital for various universal benefits and welfare services.

- Thirdly, it has to articulate credible organizational models for efficient and responsive delivery. This may involve the use of quasi-markets, incentive structures and better models of accounting and performance indicators. Ultimately what matters is that these models deliver the promised ends.

- Fourthly, it has to explain how it is to be controlled by its users. This is where the consumerist ethos of the 1990s and beyond is unlikely to be long satisfied by benevolent paternalism, particularly when faced by potentially much more aggressive marketing strategies from publishing, bookselling and other industries.

A vision for public cultural institutions

What is the vision of society that can inspire and drive the library world, that can give purpose to librarians, justify a focus on libraries and legitimize expenditure on them?

The relationship between individuals and the group is not a static one, it changes over time and thus the responsibilities of individuals to society and the responsibilities of society to individuals change too. What these mutual obligations might be depends on how individual and group problems and visions are arbitrated, turned into priorities and implemented as shared and reciprocal goals. Thus, the rights and responsibilities deemed appropriate to nineteenth-century Britain will be different to those pertaining in the twenty-first century, although common features and value systems might still persist. Similarly, the mechanisms through which overarching goals might be achieved will be different from one period to the next.

In the nineteenth century, for example, the public library emerged both as a solution to the individual and social need and as a desire for self-improvement, as well as embodying a vision that such self-improvement could take place in an institution that was accessible and free. Once established, the public library itself created its own dynamic. It became an idea, encapsulating a vision of an improving society; it became an institution that proselytized this hope, and it became a distinct building type that, in terms of nineteenth-century aesthetics, projected that aspiration in physical form. As a result, the public library became a characteristic public cultural institution that, although locally distinctive, was bounded by a shared vision and a set of goals. The library was part of the project of the betterment of society or the "good society".

Importantly, as the collective opinion of individuals persuaded decision makers that public libraries made a positive contribution to the development of society as a whole, public libraries were paid increasingly from the public purse. In order to reach such an agreement both a moral and an economic imperative were implied in the arguments. In this way individual needs and desires are identified with broader social goals, and there was an agreement within public opinion that the responsibility for providing libraries falls on all of us as a society. It becomes a common or public good.

The development of museums, art galleries, education and public housing was similarly inspired by such aspirations, as was more recently the welfare state. Some parts of this nineteenth- and twentieth-century vision have been achieved. We are more literate as a society, although clearly not literate enough; the threshold of what is poverty has gone up and more basic needs have been fulfilled, although "basic needs" themselves are constantly reviewed; educational provision has spread, although again it may be insufficient. Other parts of that vision have not been fulfilled: individuals in society are still quite unequal and many are still not reaching their full potential as individuals.

So, more is to be done not only to meet unfulfilled goals set in the past, but also to replenish, flesh out and refine these goals congruent with twenty-first-century needs, ideals and aspirations. A sustainable, more green, more resource-conscious economy is but one example that is part of an improving society, but was not something that could have been thought of a century ago. Thus, the nature of any vision for society is constantly up for debate and review, and what this vision is defines in part what we should do and take responsibility for as individuals and what we in a sense "hand over" or allow to be "handed over" as a corporate, social responsibility.

A vision is necessary as an expression of where a society wants to go. The vision thus encapsulates society's strategy. It is a means of motivating individuals to go willingly beyond their private interests, thus submerging individual needs into a greater whole. It needs to show that by doing so, not only will society benefit, but also that "I" will benefit either directly or indirectly. For example, if Britain is more educated and clever it will be more competitive, productive and thus wealthier. Older people may realize it is still in their interest to pay for education out of taxes, because the wealth generated by the young will help pay for their pension, transport or hospital facilities.

Key features of the vision that justify public commitment and expenditure to public cultural institutions like libraries include the principle that all members of society should have the right to participate fully in it, if they so wish, and thus they need the facilities to become informed. In terms of a clarion call this could be called "the right to know". Nicholas Garnham in "The media and the public sphere" describes this well:

> The rights and duties of a citizen are in large part defined in terms of freedom of assembly and freedom to impart and receive information. Without such freedoms it would be impossible for citizens to possess the knowledge of the views of others neces-

sary to reach agreements between themselves, whether consensual or majoritarian, as either social means or ends; to possess knowledge of the actions of those to whom executive responsibilities are delegated so as to make them accountable; to possess knowledge of the external environment necessary to arrive at appropriate judgement of both personal and societal interests.[3]

Linked to the above there should be an acceptance of the idea that potentially all citizens have a contribution to make to the development of society. Therefore, for example, it is better to be positive rather than negative about the contributions that immigrants and other groups can make. Thus, unleashing the potential of individuals unleashes the potential of society and makes it more productive. "The right to know" then forms part of the moral argument for public libraries, and sees them as institutions that have to be accessible to all.

But librarians will have to change to grasp the challenge. Their philosophy of non-intervention will have to be modified in a society where it is recognized that people are increasingly confused and overwhelmed, where they find it difficult to distinguish amongst the mass of information what is central and what is peripheral, where as a result various forms of psychological dislocation become ever more prevalent. As professionals, librarians will have to be more proactive in identifying more precisely the knowledge needs of their client groups and they will, therefore, to some extent have to take on board more strongly the "ethos" of economic development.

More specifically, the public library service should thus be a network of institutions that provide comprehensive access to published books, audio-visual and computer-based materials. It is a storehouse of our cultural legacy, and beyond being a store of knowledge, it is also a public domain – a place where people can enter freely, either physically or through an electronic network. In this way the library creates publics and audiences.

Audiences of all other media are fragmenting. Witness for example the proliferation of TV channels, and segmentation according to particular lifestyle markets, or even whether one owns the appropriate receiving technology. The public library service, in contrast, has a brief to serve a "general interest", that is to serve us all whether directly or through some form of communications link-up. It is not just for the "disadvantaged", the poor, the unemployed. Only if it serves all of us is it truly public and part of the public domain. If the service is identified as providing only for specific groups, then the "contents" would be revised accordingly and the encyclopaedic nature of the library would be lost.

The library in fact has a dual project – which is both to target services to particular audiences and develop these audiences, and in so doing to reaffirm that there is a general audience that shares a general interest. It does this because the library is the store of published materials, that is materials made public and put into the public realm under protection of copyright law. Yet part of the threat of new technology is that it will change the terms of publishing and the legal framework that defines what the public realm is. If copyright relations are eventually replaced by contract relations, based on fee payments, like narrowcasting rather than broadcasting, then the public realm will be altered and diminished. The library needs to counter this threat through regulations that guarantee public access to information.

Credible rules of provision

It is essential that libraries make explicit the governing rules of provision that inform the service. Below we outline a number of principles that one might expect to inform a public library service, some key points of which are then elaborated. They would most certainly include:

- Location: because of the unique nature of the library space and its function within the community, questions of location are of paramount importance.
- Being an inclusive organization, open and accessible to all, irrespective of ability to pay.
- Stock selection processes to be made explicit and responsive to local needs and interests.
- Providing a secular, non-censorial approach to materials stocked within limits agreed by open debate and explicit guidelines.
- Provided as a local service but linked to national and international networks of information.
- Stocking a wide range of cultural artefacts including books, and responsive to new formats and developments.

– Open at times that meet the patterns of life of the majority of people who need or wish to use the service.
– Flexible in its approach to funding existing and new services, and not simply reliant on tax-based funding regimes, on the understanding that ability to pay should not preclude users from the majority of services.
– Providing services within a regime that monitors use, actively seeks user comments and criticisms, and is able to adapt easily to change.

Location   The location and the siting of public libraries is central to a credible model of provision, and essentially libraries are provided in the first instance as a local service. The demographic structure of the country continues to change and yet the library network is tied to a set of historically determined buildings and sites and administrative structures.

At the same time, "local", "district" and "central" libraries are used in different ways and meet different needs. A more explicit recognition of the ways in which these different levels of the service relate to each other is needed. How can the service ensure the appropriate mix of libraries in the right locations?

In her book *Public libraries as agents of communication*, Gulten Wagner argues that the two most important issues in siting public libraries in a metropolitan region is their centrality and accessibility, "two signifiers of their solidarity with the community".[4] She also points out from her research in Australia that public library services are based upon boundaries established decades ago and are unable to respond to the demographic changes taking place in the urban scene.

Explicit selection processes   Where the "public service" model is weakest – and this is certainly true in our experience of libraries – is in making radical decisions and choices well away from the public gaze or involvement in debate. Questions of stock selection, opening hours, disabled access and priorities for spending are covert judgements and decisions rather than overt and public ones. Unless public institutions encourage a wider debate on the services they provide, invite comment, seek advice and undertake widespread consultation, they will lose public support. Some decisions and choices may be unpopular, but it is better that they are made in public rather than "smuggled" into the public realm. For example, there is no doubt as to Lambeth Council's seriousness in opening up their formidably anti-racist and anti-sexist stock selection process for public consultation. The Council has not just

157

asserted its electorally accountable "public interest" policies in book selection in manifesto terms, but has ensured that all library staff are involved in the decisions made within the rubric of book selection policy, and that reasons for these choices are clearly stated. Along then with "accountability by esteem", one might add the importance of "accountability by public debate".

Greater use of marketing techniques and greater use of qualitative assessment of services such as the use of electorally representative "focus" groups, for example, are all part of the battery of instruments that the public library is going to need if it is to keep its finger on the pulse of social change, be responsive to new interest and demands, and to involve the public at all levels in debates about library policy. The library itself has to become an "intelligent" organization as well as a benevolent one.

Networks Many library authorities have introduced "first stop" information services that integrate a mass of governmental, consumer and voluntary sector information. These steps towards a vertical integration of information within a local authority area, help to rationalize and make information provision more effective. This move can be developed and expanded by strengthening cross-authority connections – the national library network. Rather than operating in isolation, the extensive library infrastructure provides an opportunity for libraries to develop methods of provision that make much more use of this network. Library authorities may band together to provide specialist services, circulating collections, new forms of inter-library connections, and even to exert some buying power or "commissioning" ability in the cultural market. Inter-library lending is a minimal use of the national library system. The power of the library network at present seems dormant: a sleeping giant. It cannot remain so.

Opening hours In her study of Australian public libraries, Gulten Wagner has pointed out that the major portion of the opening hours of public libraries are in conflict with the 9am–5pm working day. She goes on to quote the President of the Library Association in Australia who argued that "The opportunity cost of public libraries not providing access at times to suit users . . . undermines their place in any national information plan, it weakens their community profile and undermines [their] credibility."[5] Opening hours are likely to become an important factor in the library's organizational credibility. Sunday opening, increasingly common in Australia, and more and more popular with museums in the UK, may well be on the agenda for British libraries.

Credible organizational models

Provided by local government   Public libraries have been directly provided by local government from their beginning. In many places great political battles were waged as to whether local councils should provide libraries out of local rates, but once established, library provision has become a statutory duty throughout the United Kingdom. As is evident everywhere, local government itself is now being questioned as a viable vehicle for direct provision of many kinds of services. Conservative governments have with increasing determination asserted the inefficient, paternalistic, bureaucratic deficiencies of local authority provision, and many traditional services – housing, education, leisure – have been opened up to private tendering, or put out to autonomous trusts, community associations and other independent bodies.

Would public libraries flourish outside of local government control? There is of course no definitive answer or predictive model that in advance could assert whether or not they could. Yet they must address the strongest criticism of traditional public provision that it has been based often on "producer" interests (on the professional skills, conditions and interests of the people who work in them), rather than on "consumer" interests (that is to say of the people who pay for and actually use them). It is likely that a variety of models of provision will develop over the next decades, but it has to be said that given the general "success" of the public library as a cultural institution throughout its long history, the arguments for completely removing it from local government control would have to be much stronger than the arguments for retaining it there.

Organizational culture   Librarianship has a strong organizational culture – and that is part of its problem. It has a powerful sense of its own skills and professional interests, and this has made it less responsive to consumer or wider social interests than other kinds of services or industries. This problem is exacerbated by the fact that within the library profession itself – and within its organizing body, the Library Association – public librarians are in a minority and have not fully asserted the distinctive attributes, particularly educational, social and cultural, of their own unique service. This must become a priority. Just as the polytechnics in the 1970s and 1980s moved out of the shadow of the universities to become significantly different and even more dynamic institutions of higher education, so public librarians must move their service out of the shadow of the academic and commercial library world, to argue the case for the public library service as *sui generis* and of vital future importance.

But within the public library itself there are other issues. How are users of libraries to respond to library staff and how do library staff present or interpret the library for the benefit of users? These are important questions linked to the future organizational structure of the library service. In most libraries a division occurs between reception or customer service staff and the librarian. And yet this division is not made clear to users who commonly think of the librarian as the person stamping books. The skill of the librarian is often invisible to users.

To the outsider, the service seems decidedly broken-backed professionally, with staff rigidly divided into "professional librarians" and a larger, less skilled army of "library assistants". This hierarchical and essentially two-class system seems wholly inflexible and inappropriate to modern conditions. Of course many libraries have adapted to more flexible forms of staffing, but this has not been communicated to the wider public. The fact that librarians continue to assert the absolute difference between librarians and library assistants, and indeed often "blame" the public for not being aware of this difference, shows how deep the problem is. Flexibility of skills, teamwork, fluid staffing structures and "flat" organizational models are likely to be more responsive to public needs than traditional binary "skilled" and "unskilled" models of staffing.

These problems are compounded by the fact that the library labour force is overwhelmingly female. One writer has suggested that the predominance of women supports the library's role as a nurturing institution of the state and that this can conflict with the masculine "signifiers" of a high-tech information age. Thus, there is a conflict between the domesticity inside the library and an external image that must attract attention on a national stage. This is an area of crucial importance to the library's own vision and image. For, given the great demographic shifts in the workplace towards part-time work and the new predominance of women workers, librarians have to decide whether they wish to meet these demographic shifts in a convivial, supportive and enabling way, or hide behind a more defensive, male-oriented, hi-tech public profile.

The obstacles to often necessary organizational innovation come in different shapes and forms. Most obstacles are generated by organizational and bureaucratic mentalities, cultures, traditions and histories, as well as by rigid frameworks of established professional disciplines and hierarchies.

Incorporating the kind of responsiveness and adaptability now necessary into public sector management is problematic for a number of good
reasons, and the challenge is to see how new forms of organization can
be introduced while maintaining a public service ethos. Public sector
managers are accountable to public officials who in turn are accountable
to electorates. Obviously the need to be accountable can and indeed
does slow down the pace of response to problems, which tends to be
faster in private enterprises than in local authorities. On the other hand, a
radical democratic approach to accountability could turn this potential
liability into an asset by creating channels for a good flow of ideas from
the grassroots to politicians and to public servants. In practice this
happens rarely and in a limited way, because politicians and officers are
afraid of raising public expectations that then cannot be met with adequate resources. In some cases, they may also be afraid of this process
leading to their own legitimacy being questioned and to the emergence
of alternative power structures.

Secondly, one of the central duties of public management is to regu-
late economic and social life in order to ensure a peaceful, civilized coexistence of often divergent and competing interests and to protect and
enhance the common good. This function usually takes the form of complex rules, regulations and controls. A bureaucratic system is necessary
for the administration of controls and regulations, which are often not
sufficiently flexible, fixed for a long period of time and do not adapt to
changing circumstances. Generally this bureaucratic approach has considerable weight within local authorities, and it is not uncommon that
this culture pervades and imbues the whole organization. Bureaucracy
and responsiveness are not good handmaidens.

Thirdly, as the cliché goes: "If it ain't broke don't fix it." Like many
other examples of conventional wisdom, this saying has some truth, but
in the context of the contemporary situation in public libraries and other
public cultural institutions it does more harm than good. It means that
issues are only addressed when they emerge as problems. Responses, as
a consequence, are defined by the problems themselves and do not
explore all other alternatives. The nature and speed of change in the environments in which libraries have to operate mean that policy makers increasingly will have to be forward looking, recognize problems in
advance and indeed ponder on issues that at present do not appear
as problematic. It is dangerous to let libraries reach breaking point;
trends need to be monitored accurately in order to detect seemingly

insignificant changes that in the long run may lead to a problem. More-over, the competitive situation that libraries find themselves in increasingly depends on quality, which can only be improved through ongoing reflection on problems, emerging problems and non-problems.

Paying for the public library   Over time, the idea of the "public" has tended to be seen as provision paid for centrally by the state out of the public purse through general taxation for the benefit of all citizens. On the basis of public policy it is decided that certain aspects of our lives should be handled in this way – roads, hospitals and education are some examples. This is because it is either more complicated, expensive and less efficient to gather resources from individuals in any other way, or more importantly because the services offered are seen as a fundamental right or social good. These goods and services are then universally provided and seemingly free. They are in fact not free, it is only that there is no direct charge to the user only an indirect one.

What a fundamental right or social good is is continually contested over time. During the course of the nineteenth century, it became unarguable that access to knowledge (and therefore books of learning) was justifiably paid through general taxation, because the result of better-educated people and more-informed people was of general value for the country as a whole. The same applied to hospital care and other services provided by the welfare state in the post-war period.

The reassessment of the role of the state over the last decade has led to questions over whether the state or other public sector bodies as arbiters of expenditure are the suitable vehicles to distribute and deliver public good services whether they are used by the whole of the population or not. This raises the issue of how appropriate it is to separate the public funding of services from the carrying-out of those same services.

There has been a movement to provide services through the market, such as in compulsory competitive tendering, or on the basis of the individual's right to choose. However, the effects of this marketization are beginning to show – the market cannot be the only guarantor of public cultural rights. In a market-based system, those with more resources are going to have greater access to "goods" formerly defined as "public".

As we turn to the twenty-first century, we are thus in the position where the state and public authorities are somewhat discredited as neutral and efficient distributors of public goods and are thus unlikely, in their current form, to reassert their role as arbiters, controllers and dispensers. Equally, the market cannot provide those services.

This raises two fundamental questions:
- What are the agreed public goods, for which it is justified to apply general taxation for the benefit of potentially all citizens?
- What is the mechanism by which these goods should be paid?

There are essentially three sources of funding – the public sector in its various guises, the business sector and payments by users.

In the future, one source will still be through general taxation, but it is likely to be less than at present. Historically, public libraries have been funded nearly totally by central funds. In the future, the proportions between public, private and user contributions may change to something like 60%, 20% and 20% respectively. The form by which public contributions are gathered and targeted might also change.

Currently some part of library funding is justified more implicitly than explicitly because of the social benefits libraries provide. This has become an anchor in the argument for free access. Many of those who benefit from libraries are economically disadvantaged and thus often socially as well, but the issue arises whether their misfortune is the responsibility of the library service or some other department of state such as employment or social services. Could it not be conceived that through smart card technology the unemployed, say, receive points on a card that they can use in the library to get, for example, normally high-cost information for free while others who can afford to and are willing to pay are charged for this? In this scenario, most of what the library has on offer (books and other media) would remain in the literal sense "free" for all, but "value-added or customized services" would be free only to those in need. By this method the idea of "free access" is maintained, but the mechanism to provide it is changed. In the process it allows libraries to raise the resources they need to get out of the potential spiral of decline in which what they provide is increasingly less strategic. Would such a mechanism allow the library to provide a more effective service enabling a continual increase in quality?

A further possible change is raised by the debate on hypothecation brought into the open by Demos's publication on reconnecting taxes. Hypothecation seeks to make a closer connection between taxes and uses than the current pooling of taxes that are then parcelled out by national government. This means that specific taxes are raised for specific purposes, rather as in the USA when a local government raises resources, often via referenda, for particular projects like a sports stadium. This would be easier in the United Kingdom if local authorities had more control over both money raising and its distribution. In fact, local government control over finances in the United Kingdom is the lowest of the developed countries at below 20%, whereas in Canada it is nearly 50%.[6]

An extension of this is to tax "rent". Rent, in terms of economic jargon, is the amount by which money paid to a firm or individual exceeds the minimum necessary to induce them to perform the function concerned. Historically it has been applied to justify tax on land, and more recently to adopt special taxes on North Sea oil and TV licences. The increased importance and power of the knowledge industries has not been acknowledged by changes in tax policy and it may be appropriate to apply a special levy on knowledge providers to be ploughed back into the public library system. In this way, private sector resourcing is indirectly increased and might also become further available through joint ventures in areas of mutual benefit.

Public cultural institutions of the future will be strongly defined by their independence, and it might be to their advantage to harness funding from different sources as a means of safeguarding that independence. They will thus have to be imbued with an entrepreneurial spirit and they are more likely to be light-footed than bureaucratic, with horizontal rather than vertical hierarchies. They will be gateopeners rather than gatekeepers, monitoring and evaluating their progress continuously and thus constantly justifying their existence.

Accountability

Accountability in libraries, as part of local government provision, has been traditionally ascribed to the electoral process, to the regular judgement of the ballot box. Local government services, it is argued, are accountable because the politicians who make the policies and make the big decisions are accountable at election time. This argument has declined in many ways along with the decline in both the turnout for local elections and in the public interest in local government itself. It is now a weak form of accountability, although still a valid form. Central government also has attacked local government accountability, and the community charge (the "poll tax") was precisely an attempt to link local electoral choices with the responsibility to pay. Since some 80% of all local authority expenditure is now provided directly by central government, local democracy has been largely disconnected from local taxation, and in a way from local mandate. As central government has taken over most of the fiscal powers of local government, it has also sought to take over its political powers.

However, MORI polls conducted locally signal that library services usually remain among the most popular of all services provided by local government. This in a way is another form of accountability – popular esteem and approval. But it is not enough. For while a significant section of the population may approve of libraries and use them, other sections do not. There is still a concern within the library world for "non-users", about whom so little is known. Extending the reach of the public library, through marketing programmes, through better publicity, through a more outgoing approach, again can only strengthen what we might call the "accountability of esteem".

If the users "control" the library through their role as electors, might they not control it even more efficiently if they had direct power in decision making. These are difficult waters. For, to substitute interest group control over the more mediated electoral control could bring the library within the power of an even less representative group of people, who would assert their specific and particular interests over a wider, general interest. Many local voluntary organizations are run by cliques. User-control, voluntary management, friends' organizations, all of these have limitations of their own. And as the "consumer" model of service provision gives way once again to the "general interest" model, which it may, the library may again find a point of equilibrium.

American notions of "stake-holder democracy" may be relevant here. Stake-holders are not necessarily groups with financial interests; indeed, in providing a good local library service, the stake-holders might include:
– local authority representatives
– staff
– individual users
– local educational institutions
– local businesses
– adult literacy schemes and so on.
A coalition of such interests would be worth developing as it would make explicit all the groups who have a stake in the success of local library provision.

165

At root, however, it may be difficult to sustain the ideal of public provision without some ethical grounding: just as the very earliest public realms of the classical world were grounded in notions of the good life and good behaviour, and just as the nineteenth-century library movement based itself on particular notions of self-improvement and public good.

The task, in other words, is to tie all the various economic and administrative issues back into a moral argument about what constitutes a good quality of life: an argument that can be equally clear and meaningful to the people working in the service as to those using it.

Conclusions

We have described the public library system – historically, regarded with affection at home and emulated throughout the world – as a sleeping giant. During the 1980s, it managed to avoid the excesses of marketization, of the wholesale shift of public service objectives from benign state policy to consumer-driven services, in which taxpayers, railway passengers, library book borrowers, and even cancer patients, all became "customers", and may well be uniquely poised to take advantage of a political shift back to a more collectivist, public discourse, although obviously under new conditions and in new and more negotiated forms. But if it manages, more by luck than strategy, to avoid political and organizational disruption, then it certainly cannot avoid the challenges of technology.

In June 1994, at a seminar organized jointly by British Telecom and a group of leading British academics, Peter Cochrane, BT's Head of Research, coldly accused the academics of "being moribund". He went on to say that "The technology that is going to take you all out is already here." He wondered aloud whether the university of the very near future would have libraries, buildings or laboratories. He thought it would not. Powerful personal computers, interactive CDs, videos and virtual reality programmes would prove much more effective teaching tools than chalk-boards, fallible human beings and classrooms. Students, he recounted, were now turning down places at Oxford and Cambridge in favour of redbrick universities and ex-polytechnics that had better computer equipment. But he also concluded with some potentially comforting remarks: "We were really fast off the mark with the concept of the Open University, but that has now stagnated because it has frozen in time as a format. The future is going to be interactive, faster and much more dynamic and challenging."[7]

Time and again in this book we have drawn analogies between the very best of the Open University model and the long-standing achievements of British public libraries, and have consistently argued a much closer relationship. The future is educational, education will be a life-long process, and all kinds of new technologies and formats will be developed to aid these vital processes of individual and collective development and self-discovery. Will the British public library system – a unique network of buildings and resources, still at the heart of community life almost everywhere – be able to rise to these challenges? Or will it allow the tides of historical change to sweep over it and consign it to oblivion?

Notes

Preface

1. Comedia, *Out of hours* (London: Comedia, 1991) and K. Worpole, *Towns for people* (Milton Keynes: Open University Press, 1992).

Chapter 1

1. Comedia, *Borrowed time? The future of public libraries in the* UK (London: Comedia, 1993).

Chapter 2

1. R. Williams, *Keywords* (London: Fontana, 1976).
2. C. Calhoun (ed.), *Habermas and the public sphere* (Cambridge, Mass.: MIT Press, 1992).
3. See, for example, J. Jacobs, *The death and life of great American cities* (London: Penguin, 1964); R. Sennett, *The conscience of the eye* (London: Faber, 1991) and S. Zukin, *Loft living: culture and capital in urban change* (London: Hutchinson Radius, 1988).
4. See R. Williams, *Communications* (London: Penguin, 1962) or G. Mulgan & K. Worpole, *Saturday night or Sunday morning?* (London: Comedia, 1986).

NOTES

Chapter 3

1. D. Muddiman & A. Black, *The public library: policy and purpose* (London: Comedia, 1993).
2. A. Baier, *Moral prejudices: essays on ethics* (Harvard: Harvard University Press, 1994).
3. R. Rorty, *London Review of Books* (24 Feb. 1994).
4. H. Gardner, "Opening minds", *Demos Quarterly*, 1, 1–5, 1993.
5. Hackney libraries contain all these specialist collections.
6. P. Hoggett, *The future of civic forms of organisation* (London: Demos, 1994).

Chapter 4

1. D. Mason, *Ex Libris* (London: Adam Smith Institute, 1986).
2. Sir D. Black, *Inequalities in health: the Black report* (London: 1982).
3. Raphael Samuel's comments were made in an unpublished speech at a conference held in Aberdeen Town Hall to celebrate Aberdeen's 100 years of public library provision in 1992.
4. Reported in Audit Commission, *Library Indicators* (London: 1992).
5. Sir C. Ball, "The learning society", *RSA Journal* (May 1992), 380–95.
6. P. Heeks, *Public libraries and the arts* (London: Library Association, 1989).

Chapter 5

1. J. Sumsion & D. R. Fossey, *LISU annual library statistics 1992* (Loughborough: Loughborough University of Technology, 1993).
2. Figures supplied directly by Dorset County Council, 1993.
3. J. Sumsion & D. R. Fossey, op. cit.
4. L. England, "The public library borrower", *Public Library Journal* 6 (5), 121, 1989.
5. Figures supplied directly by Birmingham Library Service and the Birmingham University Centre for Applied Gerontology, 1992.
6. Audit Commission, *Library indicators* (London: 1992).

Chapter 6

1. J. Myerscough, *The economic importance of the arts* (London: Policy Studies Institute, 1988).

2. S. Broughton, "Crisis aftermath – a role for the public library?", *Public Library Journal* 4 (4), 85–9, 1989.

Chapter 7

1. T. Kelly & E. Kelly, *Books for the people* (London: André Deutsch, 1977).
2. T. A. Markus, *Buildings and power: freedom and control in the origin of modern building types* (London: Routledge, 1993).
3. M. Girouard, *The English town* (London: Yale University Press, 1990).
4. Markus, op. cit., p. 183.
5. Ibid., p. 179.
6. R. Williams, *Culture* (London: Fontana, 1981).
7. C. Lury, *Cultural rights, technology, legality and personality* (London: Routledge, 1993), 107.
8. A. Toffler, *The third wave* (London: Collins, 1980), 192.
9. B. McGrane, *Beyond anthropology* (New York: Columbia University Press, 1989).
10. A. Vidler, "Books in space: tradition and transparency in the Bibliothèque Nationale de France", *Representations* 42, 115–33, 1993.
11. A. Vidler, op. cit., p. 126.
12. Markus, op. cit., p. 169.

Chapter 8

1. G. Wagner, *Public libraries as agents of communication* (London: Scarecrow Press, 1992).
2. H. Rheingold, *The virtual community* (London: Secker & Warburg, 1994).
3. Markus, op. cit., p. 174.
4. H. Bloch & C. Hesse, Introduction, *Representations* 42, 1–12, 1993.

Chapter 9

1. D. Goodall, *Browsing in public libraries* (Loughborough: Library Association, 1989).
2. S. Rabkin, *Places* 8 (4), 1993.
3. K. Worpole, *Dockers and detectives* (London: Verso, 1984).
4. D. Muddiman & A. Black, op. cit.

5. Elizabeth Young (ed), *The first 25 years of Compendium bookshop* (London: Compendium, 1993).
6. A. Walmsley, *The Caribbean artists' movement* (London: New Beacon Books, 1992).
7. K. Phelan, *Libraries and reading promotion schemes*, Comedia Working Paper no. 5 (London: Comedia, 1993).
8. C. Batt, *Public libraries and new technology,* Comedia Working Paper no. 8.

Chapter 10

1. The relationship between the library building and the values it represents has been much more fully discussed in Scandinavia. See, for example, "Public buildings in Scandinavia", *Scandinavian Public Library Quarterly* **26** (1), 3–31, 1993.
2. R. Snape, "Betting, billiards and smoking: leisure in public libraries", *Leisure Studies* **11**, 187–99, 1992.
3. Committee Report, Haringey Council, 1990.
4. Cited in *Demos Quarterly* **2**, 22, 1994.
5. See *Guardian* reports on the extent of depression and other forms of mental illness. *Guardian* (15 Jan. 1994 and 19 Jan. 1994).
6. L. J. White, *The public library in the 1980s: the problems of choice* (Lexington, Mass.: Lexington Books, 1983).

Chapter 11

1. This extract from a 1991 interim report by the RSA is cited in Sir C. Ball, "The learning society", op. cit., p. 380.
2. A. Green & H. Steedman, *Educational provision, educational attainments and the needs of industry: a review of research for Germany, France, Japan and Britain* (London: National Institute of Economic and Social Research, 1993).
3. OECD report, *Education at a glance* (OECD: Paris, 1993).
4. G. Robinson, "The networked society", *RSA Journal* (April 1992), 305–20.
5. *The Economist* (Dec. 1993), cited by Sir Douglas Hague in *Demos Quarterly* (1994), 12–15.
6. *Independent on Sunday* (9 Jan. 1994).
7. T. Kelly & E. Kelly, op. cit.
8. Cited in ibid., p. 83.
9. John Bald, *Independent* (9 Dec. 1993).
10. R. M. Smith, *Learning how to learn* (Milton Keynes: Open University Press, 1985).
11. R. C. Alston, *The battle of the books* (London: University College, 1993).

NOTES

12. David Willets, *Open learning in public libraries* (London: Employment Department, 1991).
13. *Independent* (28 Dec. 1992).
14. David Hough, *Independent* (9 Jan. 1994).
15. M. Goff, Chairman of The Book Trust, in the *Independent on Sunday* (31 Oct. 1993).
16. Howard Gardner, op. cit.

Chapter 12

1. C. Batt, *Public libraries and new technology*, Comedia Working Paper no. 8 (London: Comedia, 1983).
2. D. Lyon, *The electronic eye: the rise of surveillance society* (Cambridge: Polity Press, 1994).
3. Batt, op. cit.
4. Lyon, op. cit.
5. Ibid.
6. Ibid.
7. C. Handy, *The age of unreason* (London: Arrow Books, 1990).
8. *Guardian* (16 Mar. 1993).
9. A. De Clerk & P. V. Deekle, "The future of the book", *Liberal Education*, 1993.
10. M. McLuhan, *Understanding media* (London: 1964).
11. Batt, op. cit.

Chapter 13

1. P. Coleman, *Reading the future: a place for literature in public libraries* (London: Arts Council, 1992).
2. H. Schmoller, "The paperback revolution", in *Essays in the history of publishing*, A. Briggs (ed.), 283–319 (London: Longman, 1974).
3. Ibid. p. 299.
4. J. Sutherland, *Fiction and the fiction industry* (London: London University Press, 1978).
5. P. Labdon, "Acquiring adult fiction", in *Managing fiction in libraries*, M. Kinnell (ed.) (London: Library Association, 1991).
6. R. O'Rourke, *Unpopular readers: the case for genre fiction*, Comedia Working Paper no. 7 (London: Comedia, 1993).

173

Chapter 14

1. *Daily Mail* (28 June 1993).
2. *Daily Telegraph* (26 June 1993).
3. *Observer* (31 Oct. 1993).
4. *The Times* (24 June 1993).
5. *Observer* (24 Oct. 1994).
6. *Guardian* (1 Nov. 1994).
7. P. Larkin, *Selected letters of Philip Larkin 1940–1985.* (Faber & Faber: London, 1991).
8. R. Inglehart, *Culture shift* (Princeton, New Jersey: Princeton University Press, 1990).
9. *Demos Quarterly* 2, 1994.
10. C. Handy, *The future of work* (London: Arrow Books, 1989).
11. *Demos Quarterly* 2, 1994.
12. C. Handy, op. cit.
13. D. Pearce, *Blueprint: 3 – Measuring sustainable development* (London: Earthscan Publications, 1993).
14. Henley Centre, *Planning for change* (London, 1993).

Chapter 15

1. D. Bell, *Cultural contradictions of capitalism* (New York: Basic Books, 1976), 223.
2. J. Habermas, "The public sphere", *New German Critique* 1(3), 49–55, 1974.
3. N. Garnham, "The media and the public sphere", in *Habermas and the public sphere*, C. Calhoun (ed.) (London: MIT Press, 1992).
4. G. Wagner, op. cit.
5. Ibid.
6. G. Mulgan & R. Murray, *Re-connecting taxation* (London: Demos, 1993).
7. S. Watts, *Independent* (9 June 1994).

Bibliography

Allred, J. & P. Heeks 1990. *Open learning and public libraries*. London Library Association.

Arts Council 1992. *National arts and media strategy 1992*. London: Arts Council.

Arts Council 1992. *Reading the future: a place for literature in public libraries*. London: Arts Council.

Audit Commission 1991. *Local authorities, entertainment and the arts*. London: HMSO.

Audit Commission 1992. *Library indicators*. London: Audit Commission.

Batsleer, J. 1985. *Re-writing English*. London: Methuen.

Batt, C. 1993. *Public libraries and new technology*. London: Comedia.

Bauman, Z. 1991. *Postmodernity: chance or menace?* Lancaster: Lancaster University.

Bell, D. 1979. *Cultural contradictions of capitalism*. London: Basic Books.

Benge, Ronald 1970. *Libraries and cultural change*. London: Clive Bingley.

Bloch, H. & C. Hesse 1993. Introduction. *Representations* **42**.

Briggs, A. 1968. *Victorian cities*. London: Penguin.

Briggs, A. 1974. *Essays in the history of publishing*. London: Longman.

The British Library 1990. *Information 2000*, first draft report. London: British Library.

The British Library 1991. Joint ventures in publishing and information services, research paper 96. London: British Library.

Bromley, R. 1988. *Lost narratives*. London: Routledge.

Calhoun, C. (ed.) 1992. *Habermas and the public sphere*. Cambridge, Mass.: MIT Press.

Central Planning Bureau 1990. *Scanning the future*. The Netherlands Central Planning Bureau.

Conant, R. W. (ed.) 1965. *The public library and the city*. Cambridge, Mass.: MIT Press.

Credland, W. R. 1899. The Manchester public free libraries. Public Free Libraries Committee. In *Books for the people*, T. & E. Kelly, 112 (London: André Deutsch).

Cronin, B. 1991. *Library orthodoxies: a decade of change.* New York: Taylor Graham.

Cronin, B. (ed.) 1992. *Marketing of library and information services.* London: ASLIB.

Cronin, B. & N. T. Silovic 1990. *The knowledge industries.* London: ASLIB.

Cultural Trends 1991–3. London: Policy Studies Institute.

Davies, D. W. 1974. *Public libraries as cultural and social centres.* London: The Scarecrow Press.

De Bono, E. 1991. *Practical thinking.* London: Penguin.

De Bono, E. 1993. *Teach your child how to think.* London: Penguin.

England, L. 1989. The public library borrower. *Public Library Journal* 6 (5).

Estabrook, L. (ed.) 1977. *Libraries in post industrial society.* New York: Neal-Schuman.

Fisher, M. & K. Worpole 1988. *City centres, city cultures.* Manchester: CLES.

Fossey, D. R. & J. Sumsion 1992. *Annual library statistics 1992.* Loughborough: LISU.

Gadin, P. 1977. *Literature in the marketplace.* London: Faber.

Garnham, N. 1983. *Concepts of culture: public policy and the cultural industries.* London: GLC.

Garnham, N. 1992. The media and the public sphere. In *Habermas and the public sphere,* C. Calhoun (ed.). Cambridge, Mass.: MIT Press.

Gerard, D. (ed.) 1975. *Libraries and leisure.* London: Diploma Press.

Girouard, M. 1990. *The English town.* London: Yale University Press.

Goodall, D. 1989. *Browsing in public libraries.* Loughborough: Library and Information Statistics Unit, occasional paper no. 1.

Greenhalgh, E. L. 1993. *The public library as a place.* London: Comedia.

Handy, C. 1990. *The age of unreason.* London: Arrow Books.

Heeks, Peggy 1989. *Public libraries and the arts.* London: Library Association.

HMSO 1988. *Financing our public library service.* London: HMSO.

Inglehart R. 1990. *Culture shift.* Princeton, New Jersey: Princeton University Press.

Josey, E. J. 1987. *Libraries, coalitions and the public good.* Neal-Schuman. New York.

Kelly, T. & E. Kelly 1977. *Books for the people.* London: André Deutsch.

Kennet, W. 1976. *The futures of Europe.* Cambridge: Cambridge University Press.

Kern, S. 1983. *The culture of time and space.* Cambridge, Mass.: Harvard University Press.

Killen, J. 1990. *A history of the linen hall library.* Belfast: Linen Hall Library.

Kinnell, M. 1991. *Managing fiction in libraries.* London: Library Association.

Landry, C. 1993. *What is "public" about the public library?* London: Comedia.

Langford, J. A. 1871. *The Birmingham free libraries.* Birmingham: Hall & English.

Lichenberg, J. 1993. Reading, does the future even require it? *Liberal Education Journal* 79 (7), 4–11.

Light, A. 1991. *Forever England: femininity, literature and conservatism between the wars.* London: Routledge.

Lomer, M. & S. Rogers 1983. *The public library and the local authority.* Birmingham: Institute of Local Government Studies, University of Birmingham.

BIBLIOGRAPHY

Lury, C. 1993. *Cultural rights, technology, legality and personality*. London: Routledge.

Lyon, David 1994. *The electronic eye: the rise of surveillance society*. Cambridge: Polity Press.

MacBeath, J. 1994. *A place for success: an evaluation of study support in England, Scotland and Northern Ireland*. London: Prince's Trust.

McGuigan, J. 1992. *Cultural populism*. London: Routledge.

McKee, B. 1987. *Public libraries into the 1990s?* London: AAL Publishing.

Markus, T. A. 1993. *Buildings and power: freedom and control in the origin of modern building types*. London: Routledge.

Marquand, D. 1988. *The unprincipled society*. London: Jonathan Cape.

Melucci, A. 1988. *Nomads of the present*. London: Radius.

Modleski, T. 1990. *Loving with a vengeance*. London: Routledge.

Muddiman, D. & A. Black 1993. *The public library: policy and purpose*. London: Comedia.

Mulgan, G. 1993. *Communication and control*. Cambridge: Polity.

Mulgan, G. 1993. *The public service ethos and public libraries*. London: Comedia.

Myers, N. 1990. *Future worlds*. London: Gaia Books Ltd.

Myerscough, J. 1988. *The economic importance of the arts*. London: Policy Studies Institute.

Nauratil, M. J. 1989. *The alienated librarian*. New York: Greenwood Press.

O'Rourke, R. 1993. *Unpopular readers: the case for genre fiction*. London: Comedia.

Osborne, D. & T. Gaebler 1992. *Reinventing government*. Reading, Mass.: Addison-Wesley.

Pearce, D. 1993. *Blueprint: 3 – Measuring sustainable development*. London: Earthscan Publications Ltd.

Peters, T. J. & R. H. Waterman Jr 1982. *In search of excellence*. New York: Harper & Row.

Phelan, K. 1993. *Libraries and reading promotion schemes*. London: Comedia.

Publishers Association 1992. *The Publishers Association Yearbook*. London: Publishers Association.

Rabkin, S. 1993. *Places* **8** (4).

Radway, J. 1987. *Reading the romance: women, patriarchy and popular literature*. London: Verso.

Rheingold, H. 1994. *The virtual community, finding connection in a computerized world*. London: Secker & Warburg.

Schuman, B. 1989. *The library of the future*. Englewood, Colorado: Libraries Unlimited.

Selbourne, D. 1993. *The spirit of the age*. London: Sinclair-Stevenson.

Sennett, R. 1977. *The fall of public man*. New York: Alfred Knopf.

Sennett, R. 1991. *The conscience of the eye*. London: Faber.

Shiva, V. 1993. *Monocultures of the mind*. London: Zed Books.

Snape, R. 1992. Betting, billiards and smoking: leisure in public libraries. *Leisure Studies* **11**, 187–99.

Steedman, C. 1982. *The tidy house*. London: Virago.

177

BIBLIOGRAPHY

Swedish National Council for Cultural Affairs 1991. *The library of the 1980s: Swedish public library buildings 1980–89*. Stockholm: SNLCA.
Usherwood, B. 1989. *The public library as public knowledge*. London: Library Association.
Vidler, A. 1993. Books in space: tradition and transparency in the Bibliothèque Nationale de France. *Representations* **42**, 115–33.
Wagner, G. 1992. *Public libraries as agents of communication*. London: Scarecrow Press.
Walmsley, A. 1992. *The Caribbean artists' movement*. London: New Beacon Books.
West, W. J. 1991. *The strange rise of semi-literate England*. London: Duckworth.
White, L. J. 1983. *The public library in the 1980s: the problems of choice*. Lexington, Mass.: Lexington Books.
Willis, P. 1990. *Common culture*. Milton Keynes: Open University Press.
Worpole, K. 1984. *Dockers and detectives*. Verso: London.
Worpole, K. 1993. *The public library and the bookshop*. London: Comedia.
Worpole, K. 1992. *Towns for people*. Milton Keynes: Open University Press.
Zolberg, V. L. 1990. *Constructing a sociology of the arts*. Cambridge: Cambridge University Press.

Index

access 29–30, 56, 60–61, 89, 90–91
accountability 151–66, 164–7
aesthetics 118–19
age, users 41–2
ambience 62
arts, library use 34, 36
Arts Council 83
audio materials 39
Australia 158

Belfast, Linenhall Library 56
Birmingham Central Library 76–7
books
  accessibility 60
  costs 39
  electronic 67–9, 124–8
  issuing statistics 39–40
  printing 55–6
  purchasing 81–2
  quasi-sacred nature 51
bookshops
  browsing 74, 76
  library relations 79–81, 83
  role 80–81
  staff 82, 111
borrowing, buying comparison 83–5
British Library 44, 58
broadcasting, public service 13
Broughton, Susan 48
browsing 73, 74, 75, 76

buildings
  changing nature 52–3
  costs 38–9
  design 53–4, 56–7, 58–9, 60–64
  new projects 37
  types 62–4
buying, borrowing comparison 83–5

cable-delivered information 121–2
"Care in the Community" 36, 97
carers, library support 96–7
charges 65
children 64
  homework 109–10
  literacy 52, 103–4
children's libraries
  education 90–91
  influence on publishing 32, 46
citizens advice 36
Citizen's Charter 64
citizenship 114–16
civic identity 62–3
civil society 13
classification systems 57–8, 66–8
colonialism 21–2
Comedia 3–9, 73
commercial market, library role 87–8
common good, library provision 153
community libraries 33, 63, 95–7
community projects 97–8

Compulsory Competitive Tendering (CCT) 26–7
computers 120–8, 128
consumerism 64–5
copyright 119–20
costs 38–9, 98–9
crisis centres 48
culture
  decentralization 44–5
  diversity 14, 21–2, 24, 86–7, 93–5
  local 24, 27, 79–81
customer services 61

data, information relationship 117–18
democracy, decline 22–3
department store image 65
Dewey decimal system 66
disasters, library response 48
displays 66–8
Dublin Central Library 92

education
  children's libraries 90–91
  expansion 35, 101–3
  higher 35, 100, 102
  homework 109–10
  international comparison 100–101
  lifelong learning 14, 100–111
  open learning 33, 103
  paradigm 104–5
  training crisis 148–9
  vocational 107–8
Education Act 1988 34–5, 100
elderly people, library usage 41
electronic networks 122–4
electronic publishing 124–6, 127–8
employment patterns 145–6
empowerment, information services 15
Enlightenment 19–21, 55
enquiries 112–14
ethnic minorities 22–3, 92, 93–5, 108

fiction
  computerized 125–6
  popular 130–36

see also literature
foreign language services 93–5
free market, public sphere 12, 26–7
funding 83, 86–7, 98–9, 162–4
future prospects 87–8, 143–9, 166–7

gender
  staff 64
  users 41–2
Glasgow, Mitchell Library 37
globalization 147
government ministries 47
Green Paper, Financing our public library service 43

history, key moments 31–33, 153
homework 109–10
Hounslow Central Library 63, 64, 77
housebound users 96
hypermedia 125

inclusiveness 21, 23–4
information 112–28
  delivery 120–22
  demand 112–14, 126–7
  electronic distribution 67–9, 124–6
  financial value 16, 114–15, 116–17
  librarians' role 128–9
  nature 117–18
  networks 158
  provision 115–16
  services 15
information technology (IT) 114–15, 120–8
institutions, changing role 26–36
Internet 122–4

knowledge
  definition 118
  power 116–17
  as resource 15–16, 148

leisure centres 63
leisure paradigm 104–5
librarians see staff
Library Association 47

"libraryness" 51–2
literacy
  adult 33, 101
  children 103–4
  library role 52
  printing 56–7
literature
  development 56
  library influence 32–3, 46
Local Employment and Trading
 Schemes (LETS) 110
local government 33, 62–3, 159,
 164–5
location, libraries 157
London
  Newham Library 56
  services 44–5
  Whitechapel Library 79

magazines 91–2, 93–4, 121, 151
Manchester, Central Library 58
marketization 146
mechanics' institutes 103
Mill, John Stewart 20
mobile libraries 38, 39, 96
modernization 142
monetarism 26

National Federation of Women's
 Institutes 96
National Library Week 47–8
nationalism 148
neutrality 45–6, 51, 92
newspapers 91–2, 93–4, 121, 151
non-book materials 84–5
non-fiction 126, 131
Northern Ireland 56, 92
nostalgia 6, 140–41

open learning 33, 103–9
Open University 101–2, 167
opening hours 37–8, 39–40, 158
organizational culture 159–62

paperbacks 132
philanthropy 54–5

photocopying 119–20
picture libraries 84
poetry, promotion 80
policy, development 47
politics 35–6, 43–8, 45–6
population change 144–5
press attitudes 43, 44–5, 140–42
Prince's Trust 109
printing 55–6
private, definition 11
privatization 26, 115–16
professional indemnity 115
Project Xanadu 121
promotion schemes 83
provision rules 156–8
public, definitions 10–11, 28
public image 43, 44–5, 46–8, 139–42
public interest, arguments 152–3
Public Lending Right 120
Public Libraries Act 1850 28, 37
Public Libraries Act 1919 32
public service remit 13, 151
public space 12, 60–61, 65, 69
public sphere
  definition 11–12, 90, 150
  education 14
  electronic 64–5, 69
  future trends 64–5, 146–7
publishing
  electronic 67–9, 124–6, 127–8
  library influence 32–3
purchasing 38–40, 81–2, 85–6

quality of life 146

reading, independent 104
reception desk 61
retailing, library impact 77–9
returns trolley 61–2
right to know 15, 24, 51, 89, 114–16,
 154–5
rule of reason 20, 55

sanctuary 52, 91, 92–3
satellite-delivery 121–2
security 61

self-improvement 54–5, 153–4
services, survey 34–5
shopping centres 63–4, 77–9
silence rule 51, 62
Skaraborg County Library, Sweden
  69
skills exchanges 110
social class, users 29–30, 40–41
social mobility 41
social services, support 96–7
society, responsibilities 153
specialist collections 24
staff
  civil disasters 48
  costs 38–9
  gender 64
  literary judgements 46, 131–4
  neutrality 45–6, 52, 113
  numbers 38
  organizational structure 159–61
  role 128–9, 155
  skills 82, 106, 111
  structure 160
stake-holders 165
statistics 37–8

stock organization 66–7
Stockholm, central library 58
students, use 109–10
sustainability 147

taxation policy 163–5
television 92, 121–2
tendering 26–7
tourism 78–9
toy libraries 84–5

universal provision 29–30
urban vitality 74–5
users
  customers or citizens 64–5
  surveys 34–5, 40–42, 134–5
Utilitarianism 20

videos, spending 39
welfare state 32
women
  democracy 22
  library staff 64, 160
  open learning 108
  sanctuary 52, 92–3, 95